D0340854

WINE DOGS USA

3

more dogs from North American wineries

Craig McGill and Susan Elliott

A Giant Dog book

WINE DOGS USA 3
MORE DOGS FROM NORTH AMERICAN WINERIES

ISBN 978-1-921336-29-4

COPYRIGHT © GIANT DOG, FIRST EDITION 2012
WINE DOGS® IS A REGISTERED TRADEMARK

DESIGNED BY SUSAN ELLIOTT, COPYRIGHT © McGILL DESIGN GROUP PTY LTD, 2012
ALL ILLUSTRATIONS COPYRIGHT © CRAIG McGILL, McGILL DESIGN GROUP PTY LTD, 2012
ALL TEXT NOT ATTRIBUTED, COPYRIGHT © CRAIG McGILL, McGILL DESIGN GROUP PTY LTD, 2012

ALL PHOTOGRAPHY © CRAIG McGILL, 2012 WITH THE EXCEPTION OF:
PAGE 78: PHOTO © COLIN PATTISON 2012, COLINPATTISONPHOTOGRAPHY.COM
PAGE 85: PHOTO COURTESY OF THE 'INDEPENDENT', LIVERMORE CA
PAGE 162 PHOTO © LEONARD LEHMANN 2012
PAGE 163 PHOTO © BRIANA MARIE PHOTOGRAPHY 2012
PAGES 212, 244, 246: PHOTOS © NICOLE MARINO 2012

PROOFREADING AND EDITING BY VICKY FISHER

PRINTED BY 1010 PRINTING INTERNATIONAL LIMITED, CHINA.

PUBLISHED BY GIANT DOG, A.B.N. 27 110 894 178. PO BOX 964, ROZELLE NSW 2039 AUSTRALIA
TELEPHONE: (+612) 9555 4077 FACSIMILE: (+612) 9555 5985
INFO@WINEDOGS.COM WEB: WWW.WINEDOGS.COM

FOR ORDERS: ORDERS@WINEDOGS.COM

OPINIONS EXPRESSED IN WINE DOGS ARE NOT NECESSARILY THOSE OF THE PUBLISHER.

OTHER TITLES BY CRAIG McGILL AND SUSAN ELLIOTT INCLUDE:
WINE DOGS: ORIGINAL EDITION – THE DOGS OF AUSTRALIAN WINERIES ISBN 0-9580856-1-7
WINE DOGS: DELUXE EDITION – THE DOGS OF AUSTRALASIAN WINERIES ISBN 0-9580856-2-5
FOOTY DOGS: THE DOGS OF AUSTRALIAN RULES FOOTBALL ISBN 0-9580856-3-3
WINE DOGS AUSTRALIA – MORE DOGS FROM AUSTRALIAN WINERIES ISBN 978-1-921336-02-7
WINE DOGS AUSTRALIA 2 – MORE DOGS FROM AUSTRALIAN WINERIES ISBN 978-1-921336-16-4
WINE DOGS AUSTRALIA 3 – MORE DOGS FROM AUSTRALIAN WINERIES ISBN 978-1-921336-28-7
WINE DOGS: USA EDITION – THE DOGS OF NORTH AMERICAN WINERIES ISBN 0-9580856-6-8
WINE DOGS USA 2 – MORE DOGS FROM NORTH AMERICAN WINERIES ISBN 978-1-921336-10-2
WINE DOGS ITALY – THE DOGS OF ITALIAN WINERIES ISBN 978-1-921336-11-9
WINE DOGS NEW ZEALAND – THE DOGS OF NEW ZEALAND WINERIES ISBN 978-1-921336-12-6

HEALTH WARNING: VETERINARY ASSOCIATIONS ADVISE THAT EATING GRAPES, SULTANAS OR RAISINS CAN MAKE
A DOG EXTREMELY ILL AND COULD POSSIBLY RESULT IN FATAL KIDNEY FAILURE. IN THE INTERESTS OF CANINE
HEALTH AND WELLBEING, DO NOT FEED YOUR DOG GRAPES OR ANY GRAPE BY-PRODUCT.

" Happiness is a warm puppy."

—— CHARLES M. SCHULZ

THUNDER ONE-YEAR-OLD SAINT BERNARD, DOVER CANYON WINERY, PASO ROBLES CA

CONTENTS

PET PEEVE: FLYING BUGS
FAVORITE FOOD: CHICKEN
OWNERS: ROBERT AND PAT PARKER
FAVORITE TOY: ANYTHING STUFFED AND SQUEAKY
OBSESSIONS: KICKING HER HIND LEGS AND DANCING
NAUGHTIEST DEED: DOING DOO-DOOS IN THE LIVING ROOM
FAVORITE PASTIME: SLEEPING WITH BUDDY, HER BEST FRIEND

OBSESSION: PILLOWS
PET PEEVE: BUBBLEWRAP
OWNERS: ROBERT AND PAT PARKER
NAUGHTIEST DEED: DOING DOO-DOOS
IN THE PET-SITTER'S ROOM FOR SPITE
FAVORITE PASTIME: BITING AT RAINDROPS
FAVORITE FOODS: CONFIT AND LIVERWURST
FAVORITE TOY: ANYTHING THAT BETTY-JANE CAN PULL AWAY

BUDDY

LIFE THROUGH THE EYES OF A DOG

by Buddy Parker (the ENGLISH BULLDOG)

AT TIMES I SLEEP VERY WELL and have exciting dreams about being chased by a bigger, more voracious dog than I am; or, on the other hand, chasing a chipmunk, a squirrel, or some annoying bird that always seems to fly off just as I get close. But other times I seem to sleep very lightly, waiting to hear anything from upstairs, especially feet walking across the floor. Such sounds indicate that soon my parents, my mother and my father, will be descending the steps. It will be breakfast time, and also a time when I get a big morning greeting, and several pats on the head or on my rib cage. It's certainly one of the highlights of my day, because not only are the two people I love most in life in my presence, but it means that my first meal of the day is imminent. What I don't understand is that after the morning greeting and a big wet kiss on the face or a pat on the side, they always seem to need their morning coffee before they take care of me and my younger sister. Her name is Betty-Jane, she's four years younger, and I adore her, but she seems a little dumb and dense to me at times, and not fully aware of all the ways of a real dog.

My name is Buddy, I'm eight years old, an English bulldog without a bad bone in my body. I am totally dedicated to my parents, especially my mother, whom I sit next to all day long wherever she is. In fact, it hurts me intensely when she leaves the house and always says, "Buddy, I'll be back soon." I hate those words! When I was younger, she used to take me for rides in the car, but since I got older and heavier, she doesn't do that any more, and I really don't understand why. I love riding in cars – sticking my big, fat head out the window, sniffing the breeze, smelling weird and unusual smells from houses, farms, and other people walking on the road.

But back to our routine, they make their coffee, and occasionally my father will take the time to feed me and my sister. We love eating – in fact, we eat too fast. With our big mouths and our tremendous appetites, we tend to gobble our food with a lot of air, which only means that we fart constantly throughout the day. I enjoy the smell of my sister's farts (or mine for that matter), but I do think, from time to time, especially when my parents are having dinner, that they get upset when I let a silent, very beautiful

BORED. BORED. BORED. I'M STARVING.   WHERE ARE THEY? THEY NEVER FEED ME.   WAIT... WAS THAT THE REFRIGERATOR?

smelling fart out. They don't seem to appreciate it nearly as much as my sister and I do. But we get away with it, even when my parents have many guests for dinner, which is always surprising.

After breakfast, we usually get to take a nice walk around our property. Since my parents live surrounded by a state park, we don't have to worry about electronic collars, and we're not exactly the kind of dogs who like to wander like one of my older brothers, who passed into dog heaven. His name was Hoover, and he was a huge basset hound that followed his nose everywhere, and would disappear for hours on end before returning home. We prefer to stay close to the house, although we may wander down to the edge of the woods to chase a chipmunk or, when we see one, a deer. We don't chase it very far, because we're just not built for long distances, and our ugly mugs aren't the best faces for breathing very efficiently. Truth be known, we grunt, pant, and get fatigued very quickly. After a long walk where we do our business, we come back to the house and take our morning nap. Our parents seem to be on the go constantly, with my father working in his office at the end of the house, down some very steep steps that I'm too old to master now, but my little sister goes in there to sleep with him frequently during the course of the day. I stay around the house, and if my mother is home, I will be within five feet of her wherever she goes. It's pretty clear I'm a Mama's boy, her guardian/gatekeeper, and I'm as dedicated to her as I could possibly be. I just love it when she smiles at me, which is quite often. I don't know what a dog smile looks like, but I know what my master's smile looks like, and it's wonderful. It warms my heart, and I know she loves me and would do anything for me. If she goes out (and she does often, as she has an active life), I'll force myself to take a nap, either

THOUGHT I SMELT LIVERWURST... MMMM   IT'S MY FAVORITE.   OUTTA MY WAY BETTY-JANE...

on my mom's couch, along with my little sister, or by the front door. We basically hang loose and relax until one or both of our parents come back.

Evening is probably my favorite time. My parents return, I hang around while dinner is prepared, as both of them like to cook, and if I'm lucky, I'll get a little treat or two, usually from my father, who is a softie when it comes to staring at him while he's eating. My mother hardly ever gives me anything from the table and doesn't approve of my father doing it, but he can't resist. He's an equal opportunity sort of guy, giving both me and my sister something so as not to cause any friction.

After dinner they retreat to the family room and tend to watch that big old television, which we'll watch every once in a while, too, especially something from the Animal Planet, like some barking dogs chasing something. But otherwise, we know it's not real, we can't smell any of the dogs we see on the television, or any of the animals for that matter, so we usually get bored much faster than our masters do. They'll watch it for a few hours every night, and usually my sister and I will mix it up (play hard) for about 45 minutes to an hour after dinner.

Our favorite game is Tug of War, which we play with these cheap pillows my mother buys for us. They don't last very long, usually just a couple weeks, before we end up ripping them apart, but boy, is it a fun game! My sister weighs basically the same as I do, and while she doesn't look nearly as strong, she has tremendous willpower and, like any good ol' bulldog, just refuses to quit. She's a lot of fun, and we never end up fighting because she knows how bulldogs should play. I remember my older brother, Hoover the basset hound, would play the same game, but ultimately we'd end up in a major fight. He didn't know the rules of bulldog play. He was bigger and more aggressive than I, plus he had a nasty streak in him I never could quite understand. He just couldn't play peacefully. My sister is another case altogether. She loves to play, but because she has a slightly undersized liver, she wears out real fast, so I end up with the pillow, which I nuzzle and cuddle while she goes off to sleep next to our mother on the couch.

Evenings are relaxing, and early in the evening my parents head upstairs to go to bed. I never really care for that part of the day, because it means we have to go to sleep and spend the night without them. They never invite us up, although occasionally, when my dad is traveling, my mother will bring us up there to sleep on their bed. That's one of the greatest pleasures of my life, but she doesn't do it often enough. I wonder why, but I suppose because both of us fart, and I tend to be a rather restless sleeper, moving from position to position, so my mom probably doesn't get a restful night.

In any event, they say good night to us, and what I always think is cool is that both my mother and father always give us a nice little kiss on our heads before they go off to bed, so we know we're loved. Life couldn't be better when you have parents like that. They treat us well, they keep us warm, they feed us when we're hungry, and of course they give us tremendous amounts of affection. We live for them, we'd do anything for them, and we are so dedicated to them, but it's all paid back in return. A dog's life is a wonderful life, and I can't imagine their lives being better than ours. I think my parents always wonder about the real meaning of life. If I could talk, I would tell them, as I have it figured out. It is a life of love, without bitterness, jealousy, or anger. It is a life with a heart undefiled, where good and honest intentions abound. It is, most of all, a life about the joy of living.

BUDDY WAS ABLY ASSISTED BY HIS CO-OWNER / CO-PARENT / CO-WRANGLER **ROBERT M. PARKER JR.**
ROBERT WAS BORN IN BALTIMORE, MARYLAND AND INITIALLY PURSUED A CAREER IN LAW. HIS INTEREST IN WINE BEGAN IN 1967 AND IT WASN'T LONG BEFORE ROBERT HAD STARTED TO CARVE OUT A SPECTACULAR CAREER IN WINE WRITING THAT NOW SPANS OVER 28 YEARS. HE IS THE FOUNDER OF *THE WINE ADVOCATE* AND IS THE CONTRIBUTING EDITOR FOR *FOOD AND WINE* MAGAZINE. HE ALSO PERIODICALLY CONTRIBUTES TO OTHER MAGAZINES INCLUDING *THE FIELD* AND FRANCE'S *L'EXPRESS*. HE IS THE AUTHOR OF MANY BEST-SELLING AND AWARDED WINE BOOKS, INCLUDING *BORDEAUX, BURGUNDY, PARKER'S WINE BUYER'S GUIDE* AND *THE WINES OF THE RHÔNE VALLEY AND PROVENCE*. ROBERT'S BULLDOG GEORGE WON THE COVETED 'PALME DOG' PRIZE AT THE CANNES FILM FESTIVAL FOR BEST CANINE PERFORMANCE IN A FILM FOR HIS CAMEO IN THE DOCUMENTARY *MONDOVINO*. WWW.EROBERTPARKER.COM

ALFIE

OWNER: ROSE GALANTY
NAUGHTIEST DEED:
DANCING IN THE STREET
PET PEEVE: ANKLE BITERS
FAVORITE FOOD: WILD SALMON
FAVORITE PASTIME: CHANNELING URI GELLER
FAVORITE TOYS: SQUEAKY SQUIRREL AND DUCK

OWNER: TRACI SEVILLE
FAVORITE FOOD: CAT FOOD
FAVORITE PASTIME: RIDING ON
THE STAND-UP PADDLEBOARD
OBSESSION: CHLOE THE CAT
NAUGHTIEST DEED: EATING
HIS AUNTIE'S FAVORITE SHOES
PET PEEVE: HAVING TO GO IN HIS CRATE
KNOWN ACCOMPLICES: PEYTON AND
RILEY FROM FONTELLA FAMILY WINERY

OWNER: TRACI SEVILLE
FAVORITE FOOD: CHEESE
FAVORITE TOY: ORBEE BALL
OBSESSION: THE CAT'S LASER POINTER
NAUGHTIEST DEED: STEALING AN ENTIRE
CHEESECAKE FROM THE COUNTER
PET PEEVES: HAVING TO STAY HOME
AND WALLY BOBBY JR. YELLING AT HIM

ROARK

BONES

OWNER: ASHLEY KEEVER
FAVORITE FOOD: BURRITOS
PET PEEVE: BEING LEFT OUT
NAUGHTIEST DEED: HELPING HIMSELF
TO WHATEVER'S ON YOUR PLATE
OBSESSION: WAITING FOR THINGS TO CHASE
FAVORITE PASTIME: CHASING RABBITS, DEER
AND TURKEY VULTURES THROUGH THE VINEYARD
KNOWN ACCOMPLICE: LILIANA, HIS BABY SISTER

KEEVER VINEYARDS YOUNTVILLE, CA | MUTT, 3

OWNER: ANDREW KIKEN
FAVORITE FOOD: YOUR LUNCH
NAUGHTIEST DEED: STEALING LORI'S VICTORIA'S SECRET BRA AND SHOES
OBSESSION: NON-STOP PLAYING, 24/7
KNOWN ACCOMPLICE: ALICE THE 5LB CHIHUAHUA
FAVORITE PASTIME: BEING OUTSIDE FOR AS LONG AS HE CAN

MESSI

CHLOE

OWNER: KATHY BORG
NAUGHTIEST DEED: SNEAKY BEGGING
FAVORITE TOY: BRIGHT PINK MONSTER
FAVORITE PASTIMES: SUNBATHING ON
EVERYONE'S DESK AT WORK AND CUDDLING
FAVORITE FOOD: YOGURT-COVERED PRETZELS
OBSESSION: HUNTING FOR LIZARDS, GOPHERS AND PIGEONS

OBSESSION: PINOT NOIR
FAVORITE TOY: SQUEAKY PIG
PET PEEVE: BEING TOLD "NO"
FAVORITE FOOD: ROASTED PIG
OWNERS: DON AND MARGIE OLSON
FAVORITE PASTIME: PLAYING IN THE WATER
NAUGHTIEST DEED: CHASING THE FEDEX AND UPS TRUCKS

SIGMUND

GOLDEN RETRIEVER, 7 MONTHS | TORII MOR DUNDEE, OR | 17

MOOKIE

FAVORITE PASTIME: SNIFFING FOR RABBITS
OWNER: JEREMY BAKER
FAVORITE FOOD: CHEESE
OBSESSION: GREENIES
NAUGHTIEST DEED: RUNNING AFTER RABBITS
PET PEEVE: LOUD NOISES

TOSH

OWNER: JEREMY BAKER
FAVORITE FOOD: CHEESE
FAVORITE TOY: TENNIS BALL
FAVORITE PASTIME: SMILING
NAUGHTIEST DEED: FLATULENCE
OBSESSION: HIS BROTHER MOOKIE
PET PEEVE: HIS OWNER TRAVELING

MUKI

OWNER: CHRIS RUSSI
NAUGHTIEST DEED: STEALING THE CAT'S FOOD
FAVORITE TOY: DORA THE EXPLORER SQUEAKY TOY
OBSESSION: CHICKEN JERKY
FAVORITE PASTIME: LOUNGING IN FRONT OF THE TASTING ROOM AND WAITING FOR CUSTOMERS TO PET HER

THOMAS GEORGE ESTATES HEALDSBURG, CA | SHAR PEI X 6, DOBERMAN PINSCHER 4 & BLUE HEELER X 14

FAVORITE FOOD: BACON
NAUGHTIEST DEED: BRINGING
THE LAWN UP TO THE BEDROOM
OBSESSIONS: BEAUREGARD
THE CAT AND POINTING AT QUAIL
OWNERS: TOMMY AND LILY FOGARTY
FAVORITE TOYS: TENNIS BALLS AND CATS
KNOWN ACCOMPLICES: BUDDY STEVE AND MISZU
FAVORITE PASTIME: DRUMMING PRACTICE WITH STEVE

MONTY

JACK RUSSELL TERRIER, 2 | **THOMAS FOGARTY WINERY** WOODSIDE, CA

OBSESSION: SWIMMING
OWNER: THOMAS FOGARTY
FAVORITE TOY: SQUEAKY DUCKS
FAVORITE PASTIME: DUCK HUNTING
KNOWN ACCOMPLICES: ANY CHILD OR SMALL DOG
NAUGHTIEST DEED: TURNING OVER WASTE BASKETS LOOKING FOR FOOD

TIS

THOMAS FOGARTY WINERY WOODSIDE, CA | CHESAPEAKE BAY RETRIEVER, 7

OBSESSION: GOPHERS
PET PEEVE: MONTY'S ANTICS
OWNERS: TOMMY AND LILY FOGARTY
FAVORITE PASTIMES: SNACKING AND
HANGING OUT WITH TOMMY AND LILY
NAUGHTIEST DEED: DRINKING LILY'S WHITE
RUSSIAN FROM OFF THE COFFEE TABLE
FAVORITE FOODS: CURED MEATS AND FANCY CHEESE

MISZU

POMERANIAN X, 12 | **THOMAS FOGARTY WINERY** WOODSIDE, CA | 21

las BONITAS
NAPA VALLEY

SOONIE

PET PEEVE: *BEING MOVED WHILE
SLEEPING ON A FAMILY MEMBER'S PILLOW*
OWNERS: *MANON AND JULIETTE MURPHY*
FAVORITE PASTIME: *CHASING IMAGINARY BIRDS*
NAUGHTIEST DEED: *TAKING ADVANTAGE OF
DISTRACTED FAMILY MEMBERS SO SHE CAN STEAL FOOD*
KNOWN ACCOMPLICE: *HER BEST FRIEND, TRUFFLE THE CAT*

PET PEEVE: RAISED VOICES
FAVORITE TOY: STUFFED PENGUIN
OWNERS: ART AND BARBARA PAUL
KNOWN ACCOMPLICES: JASPER AND BONNIE
OBSESSION: PLAYING WITH HER TENNIS BALL
NAUGHTIEST DEED: ROLLING IN MUD AFTER A BATH
FAVORITE FOODS: MULTIGRAIN CRACKERS AND LIQUORICE

BELLA

MISS BOSS LADY

OWNER: VALLERIE COHN

KNOWN ACCOMPLICE: BRUNO

FAVORITE PASTIME: HIKING AROUND
THE VINEYARDS WITH VALLERIE

OBSESSION: SWEEPING THE TASTING
ROOM FLOOR FOR FALLEN CRUMBS

PET PEEVE: LARGE BODIES OF WATER

NAUGHTIEST DEED: STEALING DOOR-STOPS

FAVORITE TOY: CORKS WITH WINE-SOAKED ENDS

FAVORITE FOOD: STEAMED MILK FROM THE LATTES

B.R. COHN WINERY GLEN ELLEN, CA | BOSTON TERRIER, 3

BRUNO

FAVORITE TOY: PENGUIN
OWNER: BRUCE R. COHN
NAUGHTIEST DEED: BARKING
LOUDLY AT WINERY STAFF FOR TREATS
OBSESSIONS: COOKIE TIME AND FETCHING
KNOWN ACCOMPLICES: BIGGIE AND MISS BOSS
FAVORITE PASTIMES: EATING AND FETCHING THE BALL

B.R. COHN WINERY GLEN ELLEN, CA | LABRADOR, 8

FAVORITE TOY: HIS 'OWNERS'
OWNERS: KELLY AND TIM HIGHTOWER
FAVORITE FOOD: POACHED EGGS OVER MARROW BONES
OBSESSION: CHASING BUNNIES THROUGH THE SAGEBRUSH
PET PEEVE: HEARING "YOU STAY HOME NOW AND BE A GOOD BOY"
FAVORITE PASTIME: WALKS WITH HIS HUMANS AROUND THE VINEYARD
NAUGHTIEST DEED: DRAGGING AN EIGHT-FOOT BRANCH IN THE BACK DOOR

RILEY

LABRADOR, 4 | **HIGHTOWER CELLARS** BENTON CITY, WA

SPARKY

PET PEEVE: BATHS
OBSESSION: RABBITS
FAVORITE TOY: FRISBEE
OWNERS: DAVID AND SHARON DASCOMB
KNOWN ACCOMPLICES: AMBER, WINKIE AND ZOE
NAUGHTIEST DEED: LOCKING HIMSELF IN THE CAR
FAVORITE PASTIMES: CHASING RABBITS AND BEING LOVED

DASCOMB CELLARS SOLVANG, CA | BEAGLE 9 MONTHS

OBSESSION: DAVE
PET PEEVE: SPARKY
OWNERS: DAVID AND SHARON DASCOMB
NAUGHTIEST DEED: BREAKING DAVE'S WRIST
KNOWN ACCOMPLICES: SPARKY, ZOE AND HOLLY
FAVORITE PASTIME: GOING ON BIKE RIDES WITH DAVE

AMBER

BLACKY

OWNER: MICHAEL BOONE
FAVORITE TOY: MR. HUMPIE
OBSESSION: FARM EQUIPMENT
FAVORITE FOOD: GREENIES PILL POCKETS
PET PEEVE: BEING LEFT AT HOME ON A SUNNY DAY
FAVORITE PASTIME: WORKING IN THE VINEYARD WITH MICHAEL
NAUGHTIEST DEED: FINDING HIS TREATS AND MAKING THEM VANISH

COOPER VINEYARDS LOUISA, VA | MINIATURE POODLE, 6

PUMPKIN

FAVORITE PASTIME:
HEARING THE SOUND
OF HIS OWN VOICE

FAVORITE FOOD:
CHICKEN ON THE GRILL

NAUGHTIEST DEED:
CREATING FALSE ALARMS

OWNER: JACQUE HOGGE

PET PEEVE: CLARISE
RECEIVING MORE ATTENTION

ROSIE

PET PEEVE: RABBITS

OWNER: JACQUE HOGGE

FAVORITE TOY: WHATEVER
CLARISE IS PLAYING WITH

OBSESSION: HUNTING AND
LOOKING FOR THINGS TO EAT

FAVORITE PASTIME: BEING A
MEMBER OF THE 'CLEAN PLATE CLUB'

CLARISE

OWNER: JACQUE HOGGE

PET PEEVE: HAVING HER
HERITAGE QUESTIONED

FAVORITE TOY: WHATEVER
ROSIE IS PLAYING WITH

NAUGHTIEST DEED: ROLLING
IN THE ORGANIC FERTILIZER

OBSESSION: HOARDING HER TOYS

MINIATURE POODLE, 2, BEAGLE, 4 & TOY POODLE, 7 MONTHS | **COOPER VINEYARDS** LOUISA, VA | 31

CHOCOLATE CHAI

PET PEEVE: OTHER DOGS
KNOWN ACCOMPLICE: RIVA
FAVORITE TOY: WREATH CHEW TOY
OBSESSION: BEING A TYPE A PERSONALITY
OWNERS: DR. KARY AND DAVID R. DUNCAN
NAUGHTIEST DEED: SHARING A STOLEN PIZZA WITH RIVA
FAVORITE PASTIME: GUARDING HER FOOD DISH FROM RIVA
FAVORITE FOOD: ANYTHING THAT PAIRS WITH PINOT NOIR

SILVER OAK CELLARS OAKVILLE, CA | MINIATURE SCHNAUZER, 6

FAVORITE TOY: THE DUCK

KNOWN ACCOMPLICES: LUNA, MAGGIE, SCOUT AND SPARKIE

OBSESSIONS: BALLS AND FOOD

OWNER: CHRISTIANE SCHLEUSSNER

NAUGHTIEST DEED: GETTING INTO A BIRTHDAY CAKE BEFORE ANYONE ELSE

FAVORITE PASTIMES: CHASING TENNIS BALLS AND BEING A COUCH POTATO

SHASTA

VIVA LA RIVA

OBSESSION: DAVID

NAUGHTIEST DEED: EATING A PIZZA
FROM OFF THE KITCHEN COUNTER

OWNERS: DR. KARY AND DAVID R. DUNCAN

FAVORITE TOY: ANYTHING SHE IS ALLOWED TO CHEW

FAVORITE PASTIMES: CHASING BIRDS AND SLEEPING

FAVORITE FOOD: ANYTHING THAT PAIRS WITH CABERNET

OWNER: ALAN DEWITT
PET PEEVE: LOUD NOISES
FAVORITE FOOD: CHICKEN
OBSESSION: GREETING PEOPLE
FAVORITE PASTIME: CHASING RABBITS
NAUGHTIEST DEED: SLEEPING ON THE FURNITURE
KNOWN ACCOMPLICE: SUGAR THE LABRADOR CROSS

ROXANNA

FAVORITE TOY: HIS BALL
OBSESSION: ANYTHING ROUND
PET PEEVES: VACUUM CLEANERS AND TAKING A BATH
KNOWN ACCOMPLICES: SAMMY ROO AND GIDGET THE PUG
OWNERS: BAILEY McKEON-PHILLIPS AND ASHLEE NEWMAN
FAVORITE PASTIMES: GOING TO THE BEACH AND MAKING PEOPLE SMILE
FAVORITE FOODS: BRIE CHEESE, STRAWBERRIES AND BAKED POTATOES
NAUGHTIEST DEED: CHASING SKATEBOARDS WITH OR WITHOUT PEOPLE RIDING THEM

FAVORITE FOOD: DIRT
OWNER: SALLY OTTOSON
PET PEEVE: GETTING BRUSHED
OBSESSION: TRYING TO HERD THE SHEEP
FAVORITE TOY: ANYTHING TOBY'S CHEWING ON
FAVORITE PASTIME: CHEWING ON TOBY'S EARS

OWNER: SALLY OTTOSON
FAVORITE FOOD: PICNICS
OBSESSION: FOOD, FOOD, FOOD
FAVORITE PASTIME: BEING PICNIC SUPERVISOR
NAUGHTIEST DEED: EATING THE CAT FOOD, DAILY
PET PEEVE: SOMEBODY GUARDING THE PICNIC TABLE

BEARDED COLLIE, 8 MONTHS & BEAGLE, 10 | *PACIFIC STAR WINERY* FORT BRAGG, CA | 37

ZORRO

FAVORITE TOY: PENNY
OWNER: STEPHEN KROENER
NAUGHTIEST DEED: ESCAPING
PET PEEVE: NOT BEING ABLE TO GET INTO
THE BACK OF THE TRUCK FOR ADVENTURES
OBSESSION: CHASING ANYTHING ON WHEELS
KNOWN ACCOMPLICES: ASHA, SPARTICUS AND PENNY

SILVER HORSE WINERY SAN MIGUEL, CA | LABRADOR, 8

DOGS MAKE A HOME
OUT OF A WINERY

by Eve Bushman

PICTURE THE IDEAL WINERY TASTING ROOM and the mind conjures up a wooden bar, a pour out bucket, a cash register, a couple of dusty gold or silver ribbons adorning bottles on display, and a lone wine-tender waiting for you to review his daily tasting selections.

Now add a dog and the image changes. The tasting room now has a lit fireplace framed by sofas and overstuffed pillows, a middle-aged couple behind the bar, country music, framed photos of the grounds and several more of the winery family. In the corner is a dog's bed, lined in fleece, and hanging off one edge: a rope pull toy just itching for you to pick up and see if a dog comes running in to grab the other end, engaging you in a long friendly battle.

You may mosey up to the inviting tasting bar, and within moments a cold wet nose tickles you behind the knees.

You will possibly take your glass outside on a porch bathed in sunlight, lingering over a Paso Robles Rhône blend or Zinfandel; you know that the dog is following as you hear the light tap of toenails rhythmically hitting the oak flooring. You now notice a water dish under a spout and think, dang, maybe I could have brought my dog with me.

No bark, no bite, and you've found a welcoming winery that knows the power of a winery dog.

So why do dogs matter in a winery? They matter just like they belong in any family – they become an extension of their winemaker. Think about it this way: man's best friend is also great conversation starter.

"Hello mate, nice winery you have here..." kind of trails off if the guest is new to wines, new to the winery, only drinks whites, only drinks reds, in a hurry to get to the next winery, on a mission to drink everything, looks nervous, or ... is completely out of their element.

In struts Sammy the smiling German Shepherd or Willie the wildly active Welsh Corgi to get that visitor ... a little more relaxed. The visitor interacts with the winery pooch and it feels like they're more a part of the winery. A tickle under the chin paired with a little winery intro, a scratch behind the ear for that first sip and a full pat down the length of the pup's silky back with the final pour.

And I've had it happen to me. I walked smack dab into a Wine Dog photo shoot at Silver Horse Winery in Paso Robles just last year. I ended up at the winery much longer than I had planned.

In writing this article, I called the winery for an update on the dogs. I'm happy to report that all four Labradors, the two males Sparticus and Zorro, and two females Asha and Penny, are all still living amongst the vines. Every night, when the tasting room closes, two go home with the winemaker and the other two go home with the family. Seventy-five percent of the time, there will be one of the four cozying up the tasting room.

As the Labs are on "the loose" they may lend their warmth to a wedding on the grounds, but due to this, I'm told, they have all grown overweight – to the point where guests must now refrain from sharing their treats! One other tidbit of news to report, the Labs seem to enjoy howling nightly – along with the coyotes.

If you take a trip to Silver Horse there are two items, that aren't wine, which you might be lucky enough to find in the tasting room. One is the last edition of Wine Dogs USA *that I'm told "flew out the door and sold out", the other is a handcrafted dog bed using barrel staves and comfy pads. Apparently, the Labs love their new beds.*

So, backing up a bit to my original thought, besides hanging with the Labs at Silver Horse in Paso, I want to contemplate the richness of life over my Stags Leap Napa Cabernet, pair a warm day in Santa Ynez with a Chardonnay in a glass covered in condensation and a breezy late afternoon in Sonoma with a Pinot Noir full of bright cherry flavor.

And in each scenario, there is a furry friendly dog in my minds-eye. Seated, with one paw stretched over one of my feet – keeping me warm, cozy and still while I savor the moment, and the wine. And every time he looks up at me, and opens his mouth just to breathe, Mother Nature rewards me with that built-in smile. Now that's what I call a pairing.

At times, people have been known to make an emotional buy at a winery because of the experience they had in the tasting room. Charmed by the hosts, the wine, the scenery or the family pet. The wine, of course, is the focal point, the center framed by the winery. But when that wine buyer gets home, and the memory of a tasting bar or a friendly winemaker doesn't suffice, having that wine glass in one hand, and your own pup's paw in the other, will.

So what's the real difference in adding the pup to the tasting room experience? The winery feels more like home, and a place you will be itching to return to just like a tug o' war with a rope pull.

Still not sure? Many Paso Robles wineries would have to disagree as they annually support a fundraiser, aptly named Wine 4 Paws. Napa Valley vintners support their own annual event, Canine Heroes Wine Auction. And, not to leave others out, there is Canines Uncorked in Oregon, Hair of the Dog in Massachusetts, Woof and Wine in New York, Wags, Whiskers and Wine in Delaware, Every Dog Counts in Indiana, the Poochapalooza in Washington ... and the sole beneficiary of all of that wonderful wine tasting is: our dogs.

EVE BUSHMAN HAS OVER 20 YEARS OF WINE 'IMMERSION' EXPERIENCE FROM ATTENDING CLASSES, COMMERCIAL TASTINGS, WINERY TOURS, WINEMAKER INTERVIEWS AND WINE STUDIES. SHE RECEIVED HER LEVEL 2 INTERMEDIATE CERTIFICATION FROM WINE & SPIRITS EDUCATION TRUST (WSET) IN NOVEMBER 2010, WAS THE SUBJECT OF A 30-MINUTE INTERVIEW ON THE WINE DOWN INTERNET SHOW, HOSTS WINE EVENTS FOR NON-PROFITS AND PROMOTES THE WINE INDUSTRY WITH DAILY CONTENT ON HER WEBSITE. HER OWN WINE DOG, A WELSH CORGI NAMED TYSON, IS TASKED WITH THE JOB OF BARKING AT HER WHEN SHE ATTEMPTS TO UNLOCK HER CELLAR WITHOUT HER HUSBAND PRESENT. HER WINE COLUMNS CAN BE FOUND AT EVEWINE101.COM, SCVELITEMAGAZINE.COM AND WESTRANCHBEACON.COM

SPARTICUS

PET PEEVE: HATS

OBSESSION: FETCHING BARREL BUNGS

NAUGHTIEST DEED: BEING A 80LB LAP DOG

OWNER: STEPHEN KROENER

FAVORITE FOOD: GUESTS' TREATS

FAVORITE TOYS: BARREL BUNGS AND A SMALL RUBBER CART WHEEL

ASHA

OBSESSION: HUMANS

FAVORITE TOY: ANYTHING THAT SPARTICUS HAS

OWNER: STEPHEN KROENER

FAVORITE PASTIME: LAYING AROUND AND STARING AT YOU THROUGH A WINDOW

NAUGHTIEST DEED: CHEWING HOLES IN WOODEN FENCES

PENNY

FAVORITE TOY: ZORRO

NAUGHTIEST DEED: HIGH-PITCHED BARKING

PET PEEVE: BELLY RUBS THAT AREN'T LONG ENOUGH

OWNER: STEPHEN KROENER

FAVORITE PASTIME: ROLLING OVER FOR A BELLY RUB FROM TASTING ROOM GUESTS

FAVORITE FOOD: CHEESE
FAVORITE TOY: MINI TENNIS BALL
FAVORITE PASTIMES: SITTING IN THE SUN
AND CHASING RABBITS THROUGH THE VINEYARD
NAUGHTIEST DEED: CHASING THE POOL SWEEPER
OWNERS: MICHAEL POLENSKE AND KIMBERLY MILLER
OBSESSIONS: KRAFT SINGLES AND MICHAEL'S ICE CREAM
PET PEEVE: KIDS - THEY BRING OUT HIS INNER YORKSHIRE TERRORIST

DUKE

YORKSHIRE TERRIER, 7 | **MA(I)SONRY** YOUNTVILLE, CA

STOLI

FAVORITE TOY: BALL
OWNER: KATHY FIEBIG
OBSESSION: RUNNING
FAVORITE FOOD: BACON
KNOWN ACCOMPLICE: ANYA
FAVORITE PASTIME: RUNNING, RUNNING, RUNNING
PET PEEVES: LAWNMOWERS AND VACUUM CLEANERS

OWNER: STELLA WILLIAMS
OBSESSION: VINEYARD MICE
PET PEEVE: HAVING TO STAY HOME ALL DAY
FAVORITE FOOD: ANYTHING ON HER OWNER'S PLATE
FAVORITE PASTIME: TEASING THE O'BRIEN'S FIVE CATS
NAUGHTIEST DEED: DISOBEYING ORDERS BY HERDING STELLA
FAVORITE TOY: ANY SOFT SQUEAKY TOY TO PLAY TUG-OF-WAR WITH
KNOWN ACCOMPLICE: CASEY, HER UNCLE CURT'S MINI AUSTRALIAN SHEPHERD

CALLIE

BELLA

OWNERS: DR. AND MRS. JAN KRUPP

PET PEEVE: NOT GETTING TO GO ON A VINEYARD WALK EVERY TIME HER 'DAD' COMES HOME

NAUGHTIEST DEED: TRYING TO EAT THE PARAKEET THAT BELONGED TO A KINDERGARTEN CLASS

OBSESSION: ESCAPING TO GO VISIT THE NEIGHBOR'S DOG

FAVORITE TOY: PINK TOY PURSE THAT MAKES KISSING SOUNDS

OWNERS: DR. AND MRS. JAN KRUPP

PET PEEVE: NOT HAVING DOORS OPEN WIDE ENOUGH TO WALK THROUGH

NAUGHTIEST DEEDS: TEARING UP DOG BEDS AND SPREADING THE STUFFING EVERYWHERE

OBSESSION: WANTING TO BE A 55LB. LAP DOG

FAVORITE FOOD: SKINNY COW ICE CREAM CONES

FAVORITE PASTIME: GOING ON WALKS WITH BELLA

ZOE

PET PEEVE: YELLING
OWNERS: RENAE AND BRUCE PERRY
NAUGHTIEST DEED: EATING 15 BAGELS
AND HIDING THE REST IN THE FURNITURE
OBSESSIONS: RENAE AND TENNIS BALLS
KNOWN ACCOMPLICES: BUFFY AND ROOTY FROM KOKOMO
FAVORITE PASTIME: CHASING TENNIS BALLS IN THE VINEYARD

RUBY

FAVORITE TOY: A BONE
FAVORITE FOOD: YOURS
OWNER: GUADALUPE FLORES
OBSESSION: PLAYING WITH LUNA
KNOWN ACCOMPLICES: LUNA AND MURRO
FAVORITE PASTIME: CHASING GROUND SQUIRRELS

OSO

BUTTONWOOD FARM WINERY SOLVANG, CA | GERMAN SHEPHERD, 4 MONTHS

FAVORITE TOY: BUNG
PET PEEVE: THE LEASH
OWNER: GRAHAM PALMER
OBSESSION: LICKING TOES
FAVORITE PASTIME: PLAYING WITH HER MOM AND BROTHER
KNOWN ACCOMPLICES: OSO, MURRO, NIHM, ROMA AND BEAR

LUNA

GANG of FOUR rules NAPA

Located in the heart of St. Helena, California is home to what we describe as the quintessential Wine Dogs of Napa Valley. Kelham Vineyards' famous canine JoJo Maximus graced the cover of our original Wine Dogs USA book, and if you want to experience the crazy antics of these fabulous hounds first hand, then you can do no better than to start your tour here. It's a barrel of barks.

A   MISS ELLIE

RED BONE COONHOUND, AGE: 5
OWNER: RON NICHOLSEN

FAVORITE TOY: CHUY
FAVORITE PASTIME: GOING FOR WALKS
FAVORITE FOOD: ANYTHING EXCEPT CHIPS
PET PEEVE: CHUY (WHEN HE IS BEING NEEDY)
OBSESSION: RUNNING AFTER VINEYARD RABBITS
NAUGHTIEST DEED: BRINGING DEAD RABBITS HOME

B   CHUY

CHIHUAHUA / DACHSHUND X, AGE: 5 MONTHS
OWNERS: RON AND LAUREN NICHOLSEN

OBSESSION: ELLIE
FAVORITE PASTIME: EATING THE KITTENS'
LEFTOVER MOUSE HEADS
FAVORITE TOYS: ELLIE AND HIS PET KITTEN BELUGA
NAUGHTIEST DEED: CHEWING LAUREN'S SHOES
PET PEEVE: RON'S RINGTONE
('PRINCE OF DARKNESS' BY OZZY OSBOURNE)
FAVORITE FOOD: SUNSHINE PLATTER AT LUNCHTIME

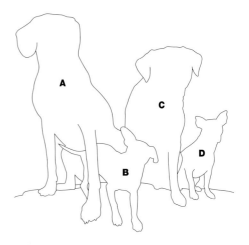

C   GABBY

FIELD LABRADOR, AGE: 7
OWNER: HAMILTON NICHOLSEN

FAVORITE PASTIME: FETCH
PET PEEVE: HAM'S WIFE, DIONE
FAVORITE TOY: ANY STICK AVAILABLE
OBSESSION: MAKING OUT WITH HAM
NAUGHTIEST DEED: CHEWING ELECTRICAL CORDS
FAVORITE FOOD: ALL FOOD KNOWN TO MANKIND

D   AL PASTOR

CHIHUAHUA / BASENJI X, AGE: 1
OWNER: DIONE CARSTON

OBSESSION: HORSE POO
FAVORITE TOY: HORSE POO
FAVORITE FOOD: HORSE POO
PET PEEVE: HORSELESSNESS
FAVORITE PASTIME: SHREDDING
ANY CASH FOUND IN THE CAR
NAUGHTIEST DEED: EATING HORSE POO
KNOWN ACCOMPLICE: RACER REX THE CAT

FAVORITE TOY:
THE DIRTY BUNNY
PET PEEVE: POODLES
NAUGHTIEST DEED:
GOING IN THE STINKY
POND THEN COMING
INTO THE TASTING ROOM
OWNER: BECKY WARNER
FAVORITE PASTIMES: YOGA
AND ENTERTAINING VISITORS

KOKOMO WINERY HEALDSBURG, CA | WHIPPET X, 4

OWNER: ERIK MILLER
PET PEEVE: LATE DINNERTIME
FAVORITE PASTIME: BEGGING
FOOD FROM PICNICKERS
OBSESSION: CHASING THE
FEDEX GUY AND TENNIS BALLS
NAUGHTIEST DEED: SWALLOWING
A CORK AND HAVING TO HAVE IT
SURGICALLY REMOVED

ROOTY

MITCHELL

OWNER: JOSH BARTELS
OBSESSION: HIS FAMILY
FAVORITE PASTIME: RIDING IN THE
CAR WITH HIS HEAD OUT THE WINDOW
FAVORITE TOYS: BALL OR SQUEAKY TOY
NAUGHTIEST DEED: PLAYING KEEP-AWAY
PET PEEVE: BEING APPROACHED BY STRANGERS
KNOWN ACCOMPLICES: ROOTY, RILEY, IRIS AND IVY

PET PEEVE: RAIN
OBSESSION: BEN THE DOG
FAVORITE FOOD: GOAT CHOW
FAVORITE TOYS: TREE STUMPS
OWNERS: THE SCHWARTZ FAMILY
FAVORITE PASTIME: SUNBATHING IN THE DIRT
NAUGHTIEST DEED: CHARGING THE ELECTRIC FENCE
KNOWN ACCOMPLICES: BLACKIE AND SWAG (OBERHASLI BOYS)

REDD FOXX

OBERHASLI GOAT, 3 MONTHS | AU SOMMET WINERY NAPA, CA

FAVORITE FOOD: BACON
FAVORITE TOY: NYLABONE
OWNERS: THE SCHWARTZ FAMILY
OBSESSION: MOVING, BUT NOT CHEWING, SHOES
PET PEEVE: THE MORNING EXODUS TO SCHOOL / WORK
FAVORITE PASTIME: PLAYING WITH HIS NEW BABY GOAT
NAUGHTIEST DEED: ATTEMPTING TO JOIN HIS OWNERS ON THE COUCH
KNOWN ACCOMPLICES: SISTER LIBBY, MAMA MARGEUX AND THE BABY GOAT

BEN

OWNERS: THE SCHWARTZ FAMILY
FAVORITE FOOD: CURDS AND WHEY
OBSESSION: BEING THE CENTER OF ATTENTION
NAUGHTIEST DEED: CHEWING HOLES IN WALLS
FAVORITE TOY: RAPIDLY UNSTUFFED SOCK MONKEY
PET PEEVE: KISSES - WON'T GIVE 'EM, WON'T TAKE 'EM
FAVORITE PASTIME: GOPHER HUNTING IN THE VINEYARD

LIBBY

OWNER: DEBRA MATHY
FAVORITE TOY: SOCCER BALL
FAVORITE FOOD: WHEAT THINS
KNOWN ACCOMPLICE: AMMIE
FAVORITE PASTIME: CHASING THE LASER DOT
PET PEEVE: BEING LEFT WITH HER BABYSITTER
OBSESSION: GREETING THE UPS AND FEDEX MEN
NAUGHTIEST DEED: RUNNING INTO GUESTS' PHOTO OPPORTUNITIES

OWNER: TOY CANTO
FAVORITE FOOD: BACON
FAVORITE PASTIME: CRUISING
AROUND THE VINEYARD IN THE GATOR
KNOWN ACCOMPLICES: ELVIS, OSA AND
SHINER AND JOE, HER HORSE BUDDIES
PET PEEVE: HAVING TO STAY HOME WITH THE OTHER DOGS
NAUGHTIEST DEED: EATING HER DAD'S SURFBOARD PATTERN

RUBY

FAVORITE PASTIME: EATING
NAUGHTIEST DEED: EATING ALL
THE NEIGHBOR'S DOGS' FOOD
THEN WAITING FOR A RIDE HOME
FAVORITE FOOD: DAY-OLD GOPHERS
OWNERS: KEVIN AND PAULA JUSSILA
PET PEEVE: ROCKY HOGGING HIS BED
OBSESSION: CHECKING GOPHER TRAPS

CHIP

MISSY

KNOWN ACCOMPLICES: ROSIE AND BACCHUS

OWNER: WAYNE PARKER

NAUGHTIEST DEED: SHOWING UP UNINVITED AT A WEDDING

OBSESSION: CRITTERS IN TREES

FAVORITE FOOD: CATERING LEFTOVERS

FAVORITE PASTIME: SLEEPING IN THE SUN

ROSIE

KNOWN ACCOMPLICES: MISSY AND BACCHUS

OWNER: WAYNE PARKER

FAVORITE FOOD: COOKIES

NAUGHTIEST DEED: GREETING GUESTS AFTER GREETING A SKUNK

PET PEEVE: CRITTERS WHO WON'T COME DOWN FROM TREES

BACCHUS

OWNER: WAYNE PARKER

KNOWN ACCOMPLICES: MISSY AND ROSIE

FAVORITE PASTIME: SWIMMING IN THE RIVER

NAUGHTIEST DEED: GETTING IN THE FOUNTAIN

FAVORITE FOOD: ANYTHING AND EVERYTHING

OWNER: KRISTY CHARLES
NAUGHTIEST DEED: DIGGING UP
FLOWER BEDS TO GET TO GOPHERS
FAVORITE TOY: SQUEAKY BACON TOY
OBSESSION: BEGGING FOR PRETZELS
KNOWN ACCOMPLICES: TET AND DEXTER
FAVORITE PASTIME: DIGGING FOR GOPHERS
PET PEEVES: NEIGHBOR'S DOG BARKING AND SQUIRRELS

OZZIE

TIMMY AKA TINY TIM

OBSESSION: FOOD
OWNER: DAWN ORTEGA
FAVORITE FOOD: TURTLE PELLETS
FAVORITE PASTIMES: EATING AND PLAYING
FAVORITE TOY: THE OTHER DOG'S HIND LEGS
NAUGHTIEST DEEDS: PEELING BARK OFF THE
PALM TREES AND EATING THE TURTLE'S FOOD
KNOWN ACCOMPLICE: THE AFRICAN SPURRED TORTOISE

MONTE DE ORO WINERY TEMECULA, CA | TERRIER X, 10 MONTHS

FAVORITE FOODS: TREATS, GARBAGE AND SOCKS
FAVORITE PASTIMES: PLAYING WITH OTIS AND
FULFILLING HIS TENNIS BALL ADDICTION
OWNERS: JASON AND ROSA LAURITSEN
NAUGHTIEST DEED: EATING SOCKS
FAVORITE TOY: OTIS' HIND LEGS
OBSESSION: HIS TENNIS BALL
PET PEEVE; SNORING

LASSEN

ROTTWEILER, 1 | **REGUSCI WINERY** NAPA, CA

OWNER: NEIL BASON
FAVORITE FOOD: CAREFULLY AGED BONES
FAVORITE PASTIME: HANGING OUT AT THE TASTING ROOM
OBSESSION: PRACTICING HIS INNATE HERDING INSTINCTS
NAUGHTIEST DEED: 'GREETING' CARS IN THE PARKING LOT
PET PEEVE: NOT GETTING RUBS WHEN HE INTRODUCES HIMSELF
FAVORITE TOY: A SINGING, STUFFED BEAR (WHICH HE HOWLS ALONG WITH)

REGUSCI WINERY NAPA, CA | AUSTRALIAN SHEPHERD X, 1

OWNER: CINDY MILANI
NAUGHTIEST DEED: STEALING THE OFFICE LADIES' LUNCHES
PET PEEVE: BEING TOLD "NO!"
FAVORITE FOOD: THE CAT'S FOOD WHEN HE THINKS NO ONE IS PAYING ANY ATTENTION
FAVORITE PASTIME: CHASING THE GOLF CART THROUGH THE VINEYARDS THEN DIPPING IN WINERY OWNER'S POOL TO COOL OFF
KNOWN ACCOMPLICES: LASSEN, JACK, BUCK, BAILEY, SAM, STOCKTON THE CAT, SAWYER AND ED

OTIS PARKER

"*I've seen a look in dogs' eyes,
a quickly vanishing look of amazed
contempt, and I am convinced that
basically dogs think humans are nuts*"

—— JOHN STEINBECK

THE DAMN WINERY DOG

by Cole Danehower

DAMN DOG'S ALWAYS IN THE WAY, thought Kyle as he watched visitors step over what to him was merely a motionless mongrel heaped in the middle of the tasting room entrance.

"Angie, can you get that dog out of the doorway for chrissake?" he called out to the woman behind the tasting counter. "People have to step over it just to get in the door."

A couple who were just coming in the room heard him and bent down to pet the dog.

"Oh no, he's just fine, don't bother him, it's okay," said the woman as the pair petted, patted, and cooed over the dog, who raised his head in greeting and gave an appreciative tail wag.

"Jeez," muttered Kyle, and turned back into his office to get some real work done. When he emerged an hour later he nearly fell to the ground trying to step over the dog, who now was lying on the threshold between his office and the tasting room. "Angie ... can you pleeease get this damn dog out of here?"

* * *

The winery staff were pretty sure the dog had been deliberately abandoned. They didn't like to think it had been one of their customers because they wanted to believe better of their clientele. They were a high end winery, after all, with a pretty stiff tasting fee, and they were tucked well back on a hillside miles from the main road so people had to make a real commitment to visit. Only riff-raff would dump a dog on their doorstep – and the winery didn't deal in riff-raff.

Nevertheless, the dog just showed up one rainy winter day, slinking into the tasting room with an air of cold soaked confusion, wary of the people inside but seeming to seek out their protection. The tasting room staff agreed he couldn't have been a random stray. Though collarless, he looked well-fed and cared for. His sauternes-colored, collie-like fur was unmatted and his toenails were clipped. He was clearly accustomed to people, and despite initial caution, he slowly allowed the staff to towel him off and inspect him.

As winemaker and general manager, it technically fell to Kyle to decide what to do with the dog. But Kyle was not what you'd call a "dog person." Considering the fate of an unwelcome homeless hound was about the last burden he was willing to add to his load, so he turned the whole matter over to his tasting room manager, Angie. "Just make sure he doesn't stay here" was his only mandate.

That was three months ago.

Despite ads placed in the local newspaper, Facebook posts, Twitter pleas, lost dog notices taped up around the area, notes on bulletin boards in town, and every other means of finding the dog's original owners, nothing turned up.

"Look, Kyle," said Angie firmly at the end of the process, "there are only two alternatives here. Either we keep him as a winery dog or we turn him over to the pound. And you know what happens then."

"The pound is better equipped to deal with him than we are," Kyle replied. "We've got a business to run here and a dog is not needed or wanted." Angie glared at him. "The customers love a dog in the tasting room," she said with a deliberate evenness. "A dog is not compatible with our brand image," Kyle countered, mimicking her tone, almost as a challenge. After a moment, Angie replied. "Okay Kyle. Here it is for you: If the dog goes, I go. What will it be?"

* * *

They named the dog Toby, after an old movie one of the interns liked. Someone brought in a dog bed and placed it in an out of the way corner. Others contributed various toys: a stuffed sock in the shape of a squirrel, a squeaky ball, a rope toy. Someone even found a durable hard plastic toy in the shape of a grape cluster, which everyone found oh-so-cute.

Kyle adjusted to the situation by doing his best to ignore the dog. Which turned out to be difficult, because against all reason Toby particularly favored Kyle. Wherever Kyle was, Toby was nearby. Wherever Toby was, he monitored Kyle. When Kyle worked in the office, Toby lay anywhere in the tasting room where he had a line of sight to Kyle's office door. If Kyle left to work in the barrel room, Toby got up and followed, settling into the same spot on the concrete just outside the door. If Kyle was in the vineyard, Toby followed a way behind, not too close, but ever present. When Kyle went off site, Toby laid outside the tasting room, only stirring when he heard – long before anyone else could – the specific sound of Kyle's truck in the distance.

Toby never raised his head in acknowledgement when Kyle's movements brought him close; Toby never wagged his tail when Kyle came into the room; Toby never sidled up to Kyle in expectation of a petting or belly rub. In fact, just as Kyle seemed to go out of *his way to shun Toby – even referring to him only as "the dog" – Toby likewise barely displayed any outward recognition of Kyle. Except that Toby's eyes always tracked Kyle, and Toby's movements doggedly shadowed Kyle.*

"It's the damnedest thing," Angie told one of her co-workers. "I put my job on the line for Toby, but all that damn dog seems to care about is Kyle, who doesn't give a damn for him!"

* * *

Harvest was the highlight of the year for Kyle. It was the culmination of his craft. He savored the adrenaline rush of bouncing from one vineyard to the next, watching the skies and studying the weather reports, tasting, weighing, and testing the clusters, monitoring their maturation, considering their optimum moment of pH, sugar, and flavor balance. He craved the challenge of calling the perfect picking moments, juggling the harvest crew, balancing the crush pad process, filling the tanks, tasting the ferments, cleaning the barrels, and even the beer-and-rock n' roll-fueled late-night hand punch downs and clean-ups. It was his element and he reveled in it.

"Look, just so you know," said Angie as she pulled Kyle aside from the sorting line, three days into crush, "there's something wrong with Toby."

Clusters and berries were sliding by on the conveyor as each new yellow bin was dumped into the hopper. Kyle and his crew were picking out the leaves, stems, the occasional rotted bunch, bugs and "material other than grapes," before the good stuff dropped into the one-ton fermenters lined up awaiting their cargo. He turned away from the stream of purple black berries.

"What?"

"Toby's sick. I need to take him to the vet."

"The dog?"

"Yes, Kyle, Toby. You know, the dog that pines for you?"

"Okay Angie, yeah, the dog is sick, I got that. Sure, take him to the vet. Deal with it – I got grapes here."

Kyle went back to the belt and Angie left. It's crush, thought Kyle, like I need to be bothered with a sick dog?

* * *

Early the next morning he left a note for Angie asking her to find him as soon as she came in.

"So what's the deal with the dog?" he asked when she caught up with him on the crush pad. He was looking at his clipboard that contained spreadsheets for each vineyard lot, fermenting tank, and eventual barrel destination. He had to plan everything precisely. The wrong lot going into the wrong vat could screw up an entire cuvée.

"The vet doesn't know for sure."

"Where is he?"

"The vet or the dog?"

"Well both, Angie," he said impatiently.

"They're in town."

"What's wrong with the dog?"

"Toby..." she emphasized the name, "was throwing up and had a hard time walking."

"Really?"

"He seemed weak and disoriented. He kind of stumbled when he tried to come out here to the crush pad. Couldn't stay on his legs"

Kyle looked down to his spreadsheets. "What does the vet say?"

"He doesn't know much yet. He's keeping Toby for awhile to run tests, observe him, and see if he can get a handle on what's wrong."

"That explains why I didn't see the dog around yesterday."

"Yes."

Kyle went back to his work. Juggling all the incoming grapes was always difficult, but somehow fun. It was like a huge jigsaw puzzle to him, making sure everything was managed correctly, all the incoming fruit got cleanly through the process, and that he knew which lot went where and for how long. It took a lot of concentration.

At noon he went into the tasting room looking for Angie.

"Anything new on the dog?"

"It doesn't look good. The vet says he doesn't know what's going on, but the blood chemistry indicates some kind of potential poisoning."

"Poisoning!" Kyle exclaimed. "That's crazy."

"Well anyway, it doesn't look good."

When Angie turned back to her work, Kyle took out his smartphone and did a search. A few minutes later he went back to the crush pad and found his assistant. "I've got an errand I need to run, I'll probably be back in an hour or two."

"What about the Eltone Vineyard? Are we going to pick that now or not?"

"I don't know damn-it ... you deal with it."

* * *

The veterinarian's office was uncrowded. A woman with her daughter sat in the waiting room with a cat carrier between them.

"Can I see the dog ... Toby?" said Kyle to the assistant behind the counter. "I ... I've got some of his toys here."

"Let me get the doctor," she said.

The veterinarian was a kindly seeming fellow who softly asked Kyle into his office.

"I'm just not sure what to tell you," he said. "Your dog has anuria, which means he can't produce urine, and we're looking at potential renal failure – and to be frank, possible death."

"Why? How?"

"Dogs eat a lot of things they shouldn't. Sometimes they eat things that are toxic. There are naturally occurring toxins, and sometimes there are induced toxins. I can't be specific here since the chemistry is inconclusive."

"Can I see him? I wanted to bring him some of his toys. You know ... might make him feel more comfortable."

"Of course."

They went into the kennel room and the doctor took Kyle up to a large cage. Toby was lying on his side, his mouth open, breathing heavily. His tail moved and he tried to raise his head up when he saw Kyle.

"He's not really my dog, you know," said Kyle as he knelt down and put his hand on Toby's head, "he's everybody's dog at the winery." He put the paper bag he'd been carrying down and started taking the toys out. The squirrel, the ball, the rope. The plastic grape cluster.

"He likes to play with them," he said apologetically.

"Did you say winery?" asked the vet.

"Yeah. Toby's kind of our winery dog. He really likes this one." Kyle held up the plastic grape cluster.

"Oh my God!" exclaimed the vet.

* * *

Harvest was over, the wines were barreled down, the rains were in full swing, and the tasting room was quiet. Angie and Kyle were relaxing with a glass of wine at the end of a quiet day. Toby lay at Kyle's side, Kyle's hand idly stroking the dog's back.

"The vet says to keep him on a mild diet. I guess he had to pump him full of activated charcoal to soak up the toxins, imagine that, and do whatever it was he had to do to get his urinary system working again."

"Good thing you took those toys to the vet," remarked Angie with a grin that Kyle didn't see. "Yeah. When the vet saw that grape cluster toy he got really excited, said he thought he knew what caused the poisoning and that he might be able to do something about it."

"I didn't know where to find you that day," said Angie "you were gone, like, forever. I never thought you'd be at the vet's. I didn't think you even liked the damned dog."

"I didn't think so either," Kyle said quietly. "But somehow not having him around seemed ... I don't know ... wrong, I guess." He looked down at Toby. "Stupid damn winery dog," Kyle grunted, "doesn't know eating grapes can kill him. Next harvest we keep him inside!" Toby looked up at Kyle and twitched his tail.

COLE DANEHOWER IS A JAMES BEARD FOUNDATION JOURNALISM AWARD-WINNING WINE AND FOOD WRITER, AUTHOR OF THE BOOK *ESSENTIAL WINES AND WINERIES OF THE PACIFIC NORTHWEST* (TIMBER PRESS, 2010) AND PUBLISHER OF ESSENTIALNORTHWESTWINES.COM. HE IS OWNED BY MONTY, AN EXCEPTIONALLY INTELLIGENT AND RAMBUNCTIOUS CHOW/GOLDEN RETRIEVER MIX.

PET PEEVE: PEDICURES
OBSESSIONS: PLAYING BALL AND TAKING WALKS
OWNERS: MARK SNYDER AND SANDRA NICHOLAS
FAVORITE TOY: NEW YORK RANGERS HOCKEY PUCK
NAUGHTIEST DEED: HIDING PIZZA CRUST IN PILLOW CASES
FAVORITE FOOD: UNCLE GLENN THE BUTCHER'S MEAT BONES
KNOWN ACCOMPLICES: LOUIE, SARGE O'CONNELL AND PEANUT
FAVORITE PASTIME: REVERSE FETCH (HIDES THE BALL THEN YOU GET IT)

BUTTERCUP

JAKE

FAVORITE TOY: BUNGS
OWNER: CHRIS CORLEY
KNOWN ACCOMPLICE: JEFFERSON CORLEY
OBSESSION: CHASING VINEYARD BIRDS (HAS NEVER CAUGHT ONE)
PET PEEVE: NOT BEING ABLE TO COME TO THE WINERY WITH CHRIS
FAVORITE FOOD: WHATEVER THE GUESTS IN THE PICNIC GROVE ARE SERVING
NAUGHTIEST DEEDS: STEALING BUNGS FROM THE BARRELS AND GRAPES FROM THE VINE

MONTICELLO VINEYARDS NAPA, CA   LABRADOR, 11

PET PEEVE: RAVENS
OWNER: KIEF MANNING
FAVORITE FOOD: PISTACHIO NUTS
NAUGHTIEST DEED: EATING SUNGLASSES
KNOWN ACCOMPLICE: MILES DAVIS THE SHEEP
OBSESSIONS: ROCKS AND VINEYARD CATS
FAVORITE PASTIMES: SLEEPING
AND CHASING THE VINEYARD CATS
FAVORITE TOY: ROCKS

DIZZY GILLESPIE

MICKEY

FAVORITE FOOD: BACON BITES
NAUGHTIEST DEED: HOGGING THE BED
OBSESSION: CHEWING ON HIS SKATEBOARD
PET PEEVE: NOT BEING GREETED FIRST BY GUESTS
OWNERS: ALEXIS VALERIO AND TRAVIS OKAMOTO
FAVORITE PASTIMES: SKATEBOARDING AND SUNBATHING

BODEGA

OWNERS: MATT AND ADRIAN MOYE
FAVORITE FOOD: DEAN AND DELUCA LUNCHES
(SUPPLIED BY WINERY PICNICKERS)
FAVORITE TOY: WHATEVER JJ IS PLAYING WITH
PET PEEVE: GUESTS WHO ARRIVE WEARING HATS
NAUGHTIEST DEED: SNEAKING FOOD OUT OF JJ'S BOWL
FAVORITE PASTIME: RIDING IN THE TRUCK AND GOLF CART

OWNER: VINCENT ARROYO
PET PEEVE: BODEGA IN THE MORNING
FAVORITE FOOD: LAMB AND RICE WITH A LITTLE
OF JJ'S BLEND (HER WINE) POURED OVER THE TOP
NAUGHTIEST DEED: TAPPING THE FOOD BOWL
TO TEASE BODEGA (WHO IS ALWAYS HUNGRY)
FAVORITE PASTIME: SUNNING HERSELF IN THE DRIVEWAY

JJ

BLUEY

OWNER: BILO ZARIF
PET PEEVE: BOXED WINE
FAVORITE FOOD: FOIE GRAS
FAVORITE TOY: A SUMMERLAND WINE CORK
FAVORITE PASTIME: CHASING BIRDS AT SUMMERLAND BEACH
KNOWN ACCOMPLICES: EVA AND LADY, THE TWO POLO PONIES
NAUGHTIEST DEED: LATE NIGHT VISITS WITH THE NEIGHBOR'S DOG

SUMMERLAND WINERY SUMMERLAND, CA | MINIATURE AUSTRALIAN SHEPHERD, 10 |

FAVORITE FOOD: FRESH PEAS
FAVORITE PASTIME: CUDDLING
OBSESSION: NOT BEING LEFT BEHIND
FAVORITE TOY: HER STUFFED LOBSTER
OWNERS: EMMA SWAIN AND WES JONES
PET PEEVE: NOT HAVING DINNER EXACTLY ON TIME
KNOWN ACCOMPLICES: BUSTER, MARTIN, MURPHY AND REDD

GG

FAVORITE TOY: NYLABONES
OWNERS: ANN AND LLOYD ANDERSON
FAVORITE PASTIME: DIGGING FOR MOLES
FAVORITE FOOD: HOMEMADE DOG TREATS
PET PEEVE: BEING TOLD TO GET OFF THE SOFA
KNOWN ACCOMPLICES: BUNGEE AND GUNNER
OBSESSIONS: MONKEYS, HORSES AND OTHER DOGS ON TV
NAUGHTIEST DEED: CHEWING ON ANN'S NEW LEATHER SHOES

FAVORITE FOOD: GRILLED CHICKEN
OWNERS: RICHARD AND SANDY LEPAGE
FAVORITE TOYS: BALL AND STUFFED ANIMALS
KNOWN ACCOMPLICES: LUCY, GOLDIE AND ENDER
PET PEEVE: PEOPLE NOT LISTENING TO HIS EVENING TALKS
NAUGHTIEST DEED: RUNNING OFF TO BEST FRIEND LUCY'S HOUSE
OBSESSION: BEGGING WHENEVER ANYONE GOES INTO THE KITCHEN
FAVORITE PASTIME: CHASING, DEER AND SQUIRRELS THEN SLEEPING

FRANC

BOOTS

PET PEEVE: THE VET
FAVORITE TOY: DEER ANTLER
FAVORITE PASTIME: HUNTING
OWNERS: DIANA AND RAY GOFF
KNOWN ACCOMPLICE: ROSEBUD
OBSESSION: SQUIRRELS (WILL CLIMB TREES TO GET TO THEM)
NAUGHTIEST DEED: SLEEPING ON THE BED WHEN NO ONE'S HOME

AMAVI CELLARS WALLA WALLA, WA | McNAB SHEPHERD, 3

OBSESSION: PHIL'S SOCKS
OWNERS: PHIL AND DEBRA LONG
FAVORITE FOOD: BOILED CHICKEN AND RICE
FAVORITE TOYS: BIG BUNNY AND LITTLE BUNNY
PET PEEVES: WEARING CLOTHES AND DOG FOOD
NAUGHTIEST DEEDS: WANTING TO HELP DRIVE AND
LOOKING OUT THE CAR WINDOW FROM THE DRIVER'S SEAT
KNOWN ACCOMPLICES: EVERYONE THAT GIVES HIM BELLY RUBS

PRESSTON

REMINGTON

FAVORITE TOY: BALLS
OWNER: JANET TREFETHEN
OBSESSION: MAKING SURE EVERYONE IN
THE TASTING ROOM GIVES HER ATTENTION
FAVORITE FOOD: AUSTRALIAN LIVER TREATS
PET PEEVE: PEOPLE WHO LOOK AT THE BALL BUT DON'T THROW IT
NAUGHTIEST DEED: DISAPPEARING INTO THE HILLS WHEN SHE WAS A PUPPY

TREFETHEN FAMILY VINEYARDS NAPA, CA | GOLDEN RETRIEVER, 4

OBSESSION: BIRDS
FAVORITE TOY: ORANGES
FAVORITE FOOD: YOGURT
PET PEEVE: BEING ON A LEASH
NAUGHTIEST DEED: FOLLOWING HER NOSE
FAVORITE PASTIME: FOLLOWING HER NOSE
OWNERS: HAILEY TREFETHEN AND ANDY HALEY

WIREHAIRED POINTING GRIFFON, 6 MONTHS | TREFETHEN FAMILY VINEYARDS NAPA, CA

OBSESSION: BEER
FAVORITE TOY: GINGER
PET PEEVE: SWIMMING
OWNER: ERTUGRUL SEVTAP
FAVORITE FOOD: 'ONE BEYOND' DOG FOOD
FAVORITE PASTIME: SLEEPING INSIDE THE CLOSET
KNOWN ACCOMPLICES: GINGER, EBRU AND NESRIN

ISIS

SEVTAP WINERY SOLVANG, CA | HUSKY X, 12

OWNER: ERTUGRUL SEVTAP
FAVORITE PASTIME: SNOW SHOEING
OBSESSION: REARRANGING PILLOWS
NAUGHTIEST DEED: GARBAGE EXCAVATION
PET PEEVE: PEOPLE WALKING ON HER STREET
FAVORITE FOOD: ANYTHING ERTUGRUL'S ABOUT TO EAT
KNOWN ACCOMPLICES: ISIS AND EVERY MALE DOG IN SIGHT

GINGER

COSMO MOON

OWNER: ROBERT GIBSON
PET PEEVE: LATE DINNERTIME
KNOWN ACCOMPLICE: MAGGIE
FAVORITE TOY: STUFFED ANIMAL NAMED BABY
OBSESSION: BLACK CORRUGATED DRAIN PIPE
FAVORITE PASTIME: SWIMMING IN ANY STREAM, POND OR RIVER
NAUGHTIEST DEED: STEALING THE WORKERS' GLOVES FROM RIGHT OFF THEIR HANDS

ROEDERER ESTATE PHILO, CA | LABRADOR, 2

FAVORITE TOY: SHOES
FAVORITE FOODS: CHEESE AND JUST
A FEW LICKS OF THE HENS AND DUCKS
KNOWN ACCOMPLICE: MUSCAT THE CAT
OWNERS: JANAE AND FRANE FRANICEVIC
PET PEEVES: LOW VOICES AND NAIL POLISH
FAVORITE PASTIMES: SWIMMING AND SAILING
NAUGHTIEST DEED: STEALING WOMEN'S LINGERIE

SADIE

OWNERS: KEVIN AND BARBARA BROWN
FAVORITE FOOD: BONES WITH MARROW
FAVORITE TOY: HIS TUG-OF-WAR ROPE
NAUGHTIEST DEED: EATING A CHILEAN
SEA BASS FROM OFF THE COUNTER
PET PEEVE: HAVING HIS NAILS TRIMMED
KNOWN ACCOMPLICE: HIS GIRLFRIEND REAH

AJAX

R&B CELLARS ALAMEDA, CA | FLAT-COATED RETRIEVER, 6

OWNER: SHAUNA ROSENBLUM
FAVORITE TOY: RAWHIDE BONE
PET PEEVES: VACUUM CLEANERS AND PORK
FAVORITE FOODS: CHICKEN AND DUCK BREAST JERKY
FAVORITE PASTIME: LAYING IN THE SUN AND SNORING LOUDLY
OBSESSIONS: LISTENING CAREFULLY AND LICKING HIS BLANKET
NAUGHTIEST DEED: PULLING THE COUCH INTO THE DINING ROOM

SUNNY

PIT BULL TERRIER, 6 | **ROCK WALL WINE COMPANY** ALAMEDA, CA

OBSESSION: CHEESE AND CRACKERS AT 5PM

NAUGHTIEST DEEDS: EXCESSIVE SLOBBERING AND CRAWLING INTO YOUR SPACE IN BED

PET PEEVE: HAVING HIS TOENAILS CLIPPED

FAVORITE PASTIME: RIDING IN THE BOAT

OWNERS: DAN AND LUCIE MATTHIES

FAVORITE FOODS: LOCALLY MADE DOG TREATS, BACON AND PIZZA

TUG

CHATEAU FONTAINE LAKE LEELANAU, MI | ENGLISH SETTER, 4

PUTTING MICHIGAN WINE ON THE MAP

by Kelly Davis

THEY'RE KNOWN AS MAN'S BEST FRIENDS but who knew they had such a sophisticated taste in wine? The traditions of dogs roaming around a tasting room dates back as far as winemakers can remember.

Chateau Fontaine proprietor Dan Matthies says when their dog Tug isn't around, customers are always asking for him. He is the winery's official greeter. Tug has become one of the most reputable dogs around. He even has his own "Setter Cider" and is featured on Chateau Fontaine's wine labels.

Tug, along with several other dogs in Northern Michigan, are coming close to celebrity status. They spent the day posing for the camera as Craig McGill shoots them in their natural setting – amongst the wine, running through the vines or relaxing on a barrel.

The dogs aren't camera shy; with a little bit of patience, McGill and his partner Sue Elliott get just what they're looking for.

McGill and Elliott started taking pictures of dogs as they visited different vineyards in Australia 15 years ago. Elliott says, "It struck a chord with lots of people – people that go wine tasting obviously love wine, but dogs are also such an important part of wineries."

The two took their idea of 'wine dogs' international and landed up in Northern Michigan. McGill says it's the perfect job, "We get to travel, we get to play with dogs and we get to drink wine, so it's all good."

Does it get much better than that? It was a win-win for everyone involved. Dog owners were proud to show off their pets. They say their wine dogs will be great ambassadors for Northern Michigan wineries. And without realizing it, Tug and his canine friends are helping put Michigan wine on the map, while they get a glimpse of fame themselves. Northern Michigan wines are one thing, but these dogs are something else entirely.

KELLY DAVIS IS A GENERAL ASSIGNMENT REPORTER AT WDRB IN LOUISVILLE, KENTUCKY. SHE MOVED SOUTH AFTER SPENDING TWO YEARS IN NORTHERN MICHIGAN, REPORTING AND ANCHORING FOR WWTV. SHE'S HAD THE OPPORTUNITY TO MEET A VARIETY OF PEOPLE OUT IN THE FIELD, INCLUDING THE CREATORS OF WINE DOGS, CRAIG AND SUE. SHE LOVES HER JOB BECAUSE EVERY DAY THERE'S A NEW STORY TO UNCOVER AND AN ADVENTURE THAT AWAITS.

FAVORITE TOY: GUS
OWNER: DAVID EAKLE
OBSESSION: GREETING CUSTOMERS
FAVORITE FOOD: PICNIC SNACKS FROM GUESTS
NAUGHTIEST DEED: TRYING TO GO HOME WITH CUSTOMERS
FAVORITE PASTIME: RUNNING AROUND THE 40-ACRE PROPERTY

OWNER: DAVID EAKLE
FAVORITE FOOD: CHEESE
OBSESSION: HUNTING DUCKS
PET PEEVE: BELLA WAKING HIM UP
FAVORITE PASTIME: PLAYING FETCH
NAUGHTIEST DEED: DIGGING HOLES IN THE YARD

OWNER: MARIA BRUHNS
NAUGHTIEST DEED: SLIPPING
A BALL INTO SOMEONE'S PURSE
PET PEEVE: LITTLE YAPPY DOGS
OBSESSION: FETCHING ANYTHING
FAVORITE TOYS: CORKS AND TENNIS BALLS
FAVORITE PASTIME: GREETING VISITORS AND HERDING
THEM INTO THE TASTING ROOM FOR A GAME OF 'CORK'

JAY

FAVORITE PASTIME: PLAYING WITH TWO TOYS AT ONCE
NAUGHTIEST DEED: DISRUPTING PUPPY CLASS
KNOWN ACCOMPLICE: MANNY THE BOXER
OWNERS: RICHARD AND ELAINE FOHR
OBSESSION: JUMPING ON GUESTS
FAVORITE TOY: TUG TOY

EMI

THE HESS COLLECTION NAPA, CA | ENTLEBUCHER MOUNTAIN DOG, 5 MONTHS

OWNER: DAVE GUFFY
FAVORITE TOY: BONES
FAVORITE FOOD: ANYTHING BUT HIS OWN
KNOWN ACCOMPLICES: BAILEY AND MOXIE
NAUGHTIEST DEED: BEING AN ESCAPE ARTIST
PET PEEVE: THE NINE CATS THAT HE LIVES WITH
FAVORITE PASTIME: RIDING IN THE PICK-UP TRUCK

SAM

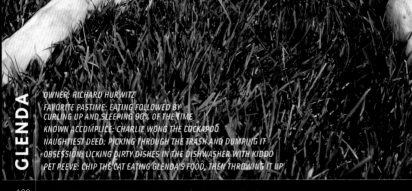

GLENDA

OWNER: RICHARD HURWITZ
FAVORITE PASTIME: EATING FOLLOWED BY
CURLING UP AND SLEEPING 90% OF THE TIME
KNOWN ACCOMPLICE: CHARLIE WONG THE COCKAPOO
NAUGHTIEST DEED: PICKING THROUGH THE TRASH AND DUMPING IT
OBSESSION: LICKING DIRTY DISHES IN THE DISHWASHER WITH KIDDO
PET PEEVE: CHIP THE CAT EATING GLENDA'S FOOD, THEN THROWING IT UP

CHIMNEY ROCK WINERY NAPA, CA | GREYHOUND, 8

FAVORITE TOY: HER TOY FOX
NAUGHTIEST DEED: EATING AN ENTIRE
HOMEMADE PATE AT THANKSGIVING
FAVORITE PASTIMES: CHECKING GRAPES
FOR RIPENESS AND SWIMMING
FAVORITE FOODS: BANANAS AND APPLES
OWNERS: ELIZABETH VIANNA AND DAVID HILL
OBSESSIONS: LIZARDS, BIRDS AND SQUIRRELS

RAVEN

FAVORITE TOY: HER STUFFED PIG
OBSESSION: BARBARA'S CHEESE PUFFS
OWNERS: BRANDON AND MICHELLE SPARKS-GILLIS
PET PEEVES: THUNDER AND BEING LEFT HOME ALONE
FAVORITE FOOD: ANYTHING OTHER THAN HER DOG FOOD
NAUGHTIEST DEED: STEALING A CHOCOLATE CROISSANT OFF THE KITCHEN COUNTER

OWNER: STEPHANIE VARNER
FAVORITE TOY: SKATEBOARD
NAUGHTIEST DEED: BARKING
FAVORITE PASTIMES: LYING ON THE
TASTING ROOM RUG AND GREETING VISITORS
OBSESSION: LISTENING TO ANIMAL SOUNDS ON TV
PET PEEVE: OTHER DOGS GETTING MORE ATTENTION
KNOWN ACCOMPLICES: VOLUNTEERS AT THE JACK RUSSELL RESCUE

DIESEL

JACK RUSSELL TERRIER, 6 | **ALTA MARIA VINEYARDS** LOS OLIVOS, CA

TROUBLE

OWNERS: HOLLY AND JIM WITTE
FAVORITE FOOD: LIVER COOKIES
OBSESSION: GREETING GUESTS AND
LEADING THEM TO THE TASTING ROOM
NAUGHTIEST DEED: TRYING TO
PLUCK A PIGEON (PIGEON SURVIVED)
KNOWN ACCOMPLICES: GEMINI,
BEAR, DIESEL, DAVID AND GEORGIA

GEMINI

FAVORITE FOOD:
HOMEMADE CHICKEN SOUP
FAVORITE PASTIME: ESCORTING
GUESTS TO THE TASTING ROOM
OWNERS: HOLLY AND JIM WITTE
KNOWN ACCOMPLICES: TROUBLE,
BEAR, DIESEL, DAVID AND GEORGIA
PET PEEVE: MISSING A RIDE IN THE CAR

A BLOOMING HILL VINEYARD CORNELIUS, OR | PIT BULL TERRIER X, 2 & HUSKY X, 7

OWNER: JESSE LANGE
PET PEEVE: JESSE'S SUITCASE
FAVORITE TOY: YELLOW PENN #8 TENNIS BALL
FAVORITE PASTIMES: TENNIS BALL THROWS IN
THE VINEYARD AND WATCHING THE GAME ON TV
NAUGHTIEST DEED: HAVING AN ALTERNATIVE DEFINITION OF PERFUME
OBSESSIONS: WINE, FOOD AND REMOVING THE SQUEAKER FROM TOYS

HERD IT ON THE GRAPEVINE...

The Lange Estate Sheltie gang just love to do what comes naturally... herding! Usually led by their fearless team leaders Polly and Lucy, these rambunctious Oregon Wine Dogs love to round up anything: squirrles, birds, each other... They spend their days playing chase around the beautiful hilltop estate, pausing only for a pat from a tasting room visitor or two. They also enjoy their 'down' time – usually in front of the TV, taking in their favorite programs, on Animal Planet of course!

A POLLY

SHETLAND SHEEPDOG, AGE: 4
OWNERS: WENDY AND DON LANGE

OBSESSION: DON LANGE
FAVORITE TOY: SQUEAKY LAMB
PET PEEVE: NOT BEING IN CHARGE
*FAVORITE FOODS: FRESHLY BAKED BREAD
AND LOCALLY MADE GOAT CHEESE*
FAVORITE PASTIME: ROUNDING UP HER PACK
NAUGHTIEST DEED: HOGGING THE TV REMOTE

B NELLIE AKA 'CHAINSAW'

SHETLAND SHEEPDOG, AGE: 4
OWNERS: WENDY AND DON LANGE

OBSESSION: BIRDS
PET PEEVE: BIRDS
FAVORITE TOY: MINNIE
*FAVORITE PASTIME: WATCHING
THE FRENCH OPEN ON HD TV*
*NAUGHTIEST DEED: HIDING
WHEN IT'S TIME FOR WALIKIES*
*FAVORITE FOODS:
ALMONDS AND VANILLA YOGURT*

C MINNIE

SHETLAND SHEEPDOG, AGE: 1
OWNERS: WENDY AND DON LANGE

FAVORITE TOY: NELLIE
OBSESSION: GOING TO WORK
FAVORITE FOOD: PEANUT BUTTER
FAVORITE PASTIME: RIDING IN HER POSH BAG
*PET PEEVE: BEING IN HER POSH BAG AND
BEING LEFT IN THE CAR*

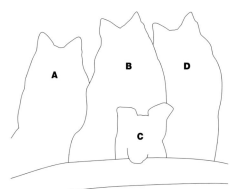

D LUCY

SHETLAND SHEEPDOG, AGE: 5
OWNERS: WENDY AND DON LANGE

FAVORITE PASTIME: DAYDREAMING
FAVORITE FOODS: BREAD AND BANANAS
OBSESSION: BREAD
FAVORITE TOY: MINNIE
NAUGHTIEST DEED: OH, WHERE TO BEGIN!
*PET PEEVE: ANYONE LEAVING THE ROOM
WITHOUT PERMISSION*

PET PEEVE: CATS
FAVORITE TOY: TENNIS BALL
OWNERS: RUSSELL FROM AND VAILIA ESH
NAUGHTIEST DEED: EATING LIVE CHICKENS
FAVORITE FOODS: STOUT CUPCAKES WITH CREAM
CHEESE FROSTING AND COMPLEX CARBOHYDRATES
OBSESSIONS: CITRUS, BALLS, GUNS AND BUNGS
KNOWN ACCOMPLICES: VAILIA, PAIGE, ABBEY AND BAILEY

HANK

HERMAN STORY WINERY PASO ROBLES, CA | GERMAN SHORTHAIRED POINTER, 4

ON THE BALL

<u>ONE-ON-ONE WITH HANK; WINE DOG & BON VIVANT</u>

by Vailia Esh

Interviewer: So, is it Henry or Hank?

Hank: *(Laughing)* It's Hank. Unless I'm being really good or really naughty, then it's Henry.

Interviewer: Where did you grow up?

Hank: In a little town called Cuyama. It's so small, I don't know if it's even a town... it's kinda desolate. I had 6 brothers and sisters, we lived in a cage outside. *(Distractedly looks away).* Oh, sorry, I thought I saw a tennis ball... anyways, it would have been a pretty boring life if my Dad hadn't stopped by one day while looking at vineyards. I was sitting off in the corner, plotting my escape from the cage, when this huge guy came in and picked me up. That was it. I went home with him that day to the beautiful town of San Luis Obispo and have been living the life of Riley ever since.

Interviewer: What are your responsibilities as a winery dog? And um, you can stop sniffing me back there.

Hank: Oh sorry, force of habit, you know. Nice bouquet, by the way... actually, part of my duties at the winery include doing a daily bung check. I also assist my Dad in assessing and surveying vineyards. I go ahead of him and make sure all is ok. I hunt along the way, to help provide for the family. I help at the winery, making sure there are no critters running about that don't belong. My main job, though, is greeting the guests who come into the tasting room. As soon as I hear the doorbell, I'm there to greet them with my ball and make them feel welcome. Hey, is that a stick?

Interviewer: No, this is my pen. What are some of your favorite pastimes?

Hank: Hunting of course, I'm a bird dog. Included in my kill list is a jackrabbit, moles, gophers, ducks, chickens, turkeys... there's a few I shouldn't mention either. I have a great affinity for tennis balls, almost at an obsessive level.

I also love to float the river. Well, I run and swim while everyone else floats. I'm the king of dominating big sticks, flushing quail, and looking for wild pigs. Are you sure you don't have a ball on you?

Interviewer: Um, no. Sorry. So, what is the best part about being a winery dog in the central coast?

Hank: Hmm, besides the amazing weather and real friendly people? Well, besides the abundance of tennis balls, this area has been making a name for itself in the wine world, so the vineyards I get to run and hunt on are pretty amazing. We travel all the way from Santa Ynez to Santa Barbara Highlands to Paso Robles. Also, folks around here do love their dogs, so no matter where we go, we get greeted with a smile, amazing hospitality, and if I'm lucky, a treat. How bout those, d'ya got any treats on you?

Interviewer: Sorry again, but I think we're done here. Thanks for your time.

Hank: Time? What's that? Can I chase it?

Interviewer: Hank, you have no idea...

VAILIA ESH WRITES VERY LITTLE, BUT IS HANK'S LOVING MOTHER. SHE HAS HER OWN LABEL, 'DESPARADA', THAT SHE MAKES AT HERMAN STORY'S WINERY IN PASO ROBLES. VAILIA CO-PARENTS HANK WITH RUSSELL P. FROM, OWNER AND WINEMAKER OF HERMAN STORY WINES, WHO STARTED HIS OWN LABEL TEN YEARS AGO AT THE YOUNG AGE OF 26 (THAT'S ALMOST FOUR IN DOG YEARS). RUSSELL AND VAILIA MAKE THEIR WINES IN AN URBAN WINERY IN DOWNTOWN PASO ROBLES. RUSSELL HAS BEEN HEARD TO SAY AROUND THE WINERY THAT THE BARRELS DON'T CARE THEY'RE NOT IN SOME FANCY CAVE OR A MILLION DOLLAR WINERY. THEY LIKE BEING DOWNTOWN. THEY'RE CLOSER TO THE PUBS AND RESTAURANTS...

FAVORITE FOOD: BISCUITS
OBSESSION: HIS RUBBER KEYS
OWNERS: NICOLE AND RYAN HILL
PET PEEVE: HAVING HIS NAILS CLIPPED
NAUGHTIEST DEEDS: JUMPING ON THE LEATHER
COUCHES AND SNEAKING INTO THE BATHROOM TRASH
FAVORITE PASTIMES: SLEEPING AND LOOKING FOR FOOD

TEDDY

PET PEEVE: BATHS
FAVORITE TOY: OTTO
NAUGHTIEST DEED: SAMPLING LOW
HANGING FRUIT FROM THE VINES
OWNERS: ELLEN AND GARY LUCHTEL
OBSESSION: WHATEVER YOU'RE DOING
FAVORITE PASTIME: RIDING AROUND IN THE GOLF CART

PET PEEVE: BEING TOLD TO DO
ANYTHING HE DOESN'T WANT TO DO
OWNERS: ELLEN AND GARY LUCHTEL
FAVORITE FOODS: RIVA'S LEFTOVERS
AND THE NEIGHBOR'S CAT FOOD
OBSESSION: CHECKING ON FRUIT STATUS
NAUGHTIEST DEED: CHASING (AND CATCHING) RABBITS

JACKSON

FAVORITE TOY: BALLS
AND MORE BALLS

NAUGHTIEST DEED: SNEAKING
INTO BRIAN AND CLAUDIA'S BED
AND WAKING THEM UP

PET PEEVE: BALLS GETTING
STUCK UNDER THE COUCH

OWNERS: THE FLEURY FAMILY

RILEY

FAVORITE TOY: A BONE

PET PEEVE: LOSING HIS BONE
TO HIS BROTHER BAILEY

OWNERS: THE FLEURY FAMILY

FAVORITE FOOD: RIB EYE BONES

FAVORITE PASTIME: EATING BONES

NAUGHTIEST DEED: BURYING BONES

BAILEY

FAVORITE FOOD:
CHICKEN AND WHITE RICE

FAVORITE PASTIME:
WRESTLING WITH THE CATS

NAUGHTIEST DEED: EATING
HIS BROTHER RILEY'S FOOD

OWNERS: THE FLEURY FAMILY

OBSESSION: BARKING AT CATS

MOLLY

FAVORITE FOOD: BISQUETS
FAVORITE TOY: WILLIE THE WEASEL
OBSESSION: PLAYING WITH SADIE
OWNERS: JIMMY AND SHELLY ZANOLI
KNOWN ACCOMPLICES: SADIE AND BELLA
PET PEEVE: NOT HAVING ENOUGH PLAYTIME
NAUGHTIEST DEED: RUNNING OFF WITH SOCKS

BELLA LUNA WINERY, TEMPLETON, CA | GOLDENDOODLE, 4 MONTHS

CLEMENTINE

FAVORITE PASTIME: HERDING HENS
NAUGHTIEST DEED: CHASING THE CHICKENS
PET PEEVE: WHEN CLARE WORKS HER
DRAFT HORSES AND SHE GETS LOCKED UP
KNOWN ACCOMPLICES: ALL THE BIG
TABLE FARM PIGS, CHICKENS AND COWS
OBSESSION: THE SQUIRREL IN THE WOOD PILE
OWNERS: CLARE CARVER AND BRIAN MARCY

LEVI

OBSESSION: CLARE'S UNDERWEAR
FAVORITE TOY: CLARE'S UNDERWEAR
OWNERS: CLARE CARVER AND BRIAN MARCY
NAUGHTIEST DEED: CHEWING CLARE'S UNDERWEAR
FAVORITE PASTIME: CHEWING CLARE'S UNDERWEAR
PET PEEVE: HAVING CLARE'S UNDERWEAR TAKEN AWAY

COLE

OWNER: LIZ ROBASCIOTTI
KNOWN ACCOMPLICES: PICNICKERS
PET PEEVE: PEOPLE NOT FEEDING HIM
NAUGHTIEST DEED: STEALING PEOPLE'S FOOD
OBSESSIONS: PICNICKING AND HUNTING FOR KOI
FAVORITE PASTIMES: EATING AND CHECKING VISITORS FOR FOOD

BIANCHI WINERY PASO ROBLES, CA | BOXER X, 9

OWNER: JILL RYAN
OBSESSION: TREAT?
DID SOMEONE SAY TREAT?
FAVORITE FOOD: THE BARN CAT'S MEOW MIX
NAUGHTIEST DEED: EATING THE EXTREMITIES
OFF A THAWING THANKSGIVING DAY TURKEY
KNOWN ACCOMPLICES: 18 HORSES, 6 SHEEP,
4 GOATS, SOME DUCKS AND TOO MANY CHICKENS
FAVORITE PASTIME: MOREL MUSHROOM HUNTING

ZOË

TUCKER

FAVORITE FOOD: FILET MIGNON
FLAVORED CHOW WITH BAKED
POTATO, NO BUTTER AND KIBBLES
FAVORITE PASTIME: ESCORTING PURVEYORS
OF FINE FOOD, WINE AND ART TO THE TASTING ROOM
OBSESSION: HANGING OUT WITH TOO SHAY THE CAT
OWNERS: KATHLEEN CONWAY AND GREG CROPPER

OBSESSION: POODLE SKIRTS
FAVORITE PASTIMES: CHASING
PEOPLE AND NIBBLING BAGUETTES
FAVORITE FOOD: SLOW-ROASTED CHICKEN,
RICE AND KIBBLES WITH PASO ROBLES FINEST
OWNERS: KATHLEEN CONWAY AND GREG CROPPER

CHASE

CARMODY McKNIGHT ESTATE PASO ROBLES, CA | STANDARD POODLES, 4

PET PEEVE: SIRENS
OBSESSION: DINNER TIME
OWNERS: BROCK AND MICHELLE WATERMAN
NAUGHTIEST DEED: TAKING A STEAK OFF THE GRILL
KNOWN ACCOMPLICE: HIS DEPARTED FRIEND APRIL
FAVORITE TOY: KIDS' BASEBALLS LEFT LYING AROUND
FAVORITE PASTIME: LAYING IN THE DRIVE WATCHING THE VINES GROW

LUKE

THUNDER

OBSESSION: STUBBY THE CAT
FAVORITE PASTIME: SWIMMING
FAVORITE FOOD: DUCK BREAST
FAVORITE TOY: STUBBY THE CAT
PET PEEVE: PETTING THE KITTIES
OWNERS: GLENDA AND DAN PANICO
NAUGHTIEST DEED: EATING A WINDOW FRAME

DOVER CANYON WINERY PASO ROBLES, CA | SAINT BERNARD, 1

FAVORITE TOY: WINSTON
OWNER: SALLY BUCHANAN
OBSESSION: HIS RED WAGON
NAUGHTIEST DEED: FARTING IN FRONT
OF THE WINE DOGS PHOTOGRAPHER
PET PEEVE: WINSTON STEALING HIS TOYS
FAVORITE PASTIME: RIDING IN THE RED WAGON

PET PEEVE: MORNINGS
FAVORITE TOY: SQUEAKY CHICKEN
OBSESSION: ANYTHING THAT SQUEAKS
OWNERS: RYAN BEE AND KATIE BUCHANAN
FAVORITE PASTIME: GREETING GUESTS AT THE WINERY
NAUGHTIEST DEED: STEALING AND HIDING FRED'S TOYS

ENGLISH BULLDOG, 3 & YORKSHIRE TERRIER, 1 | FALCOR WINERY NAPA, CA

PET PEEVE: SKUNKS
OWNERS: BARB AND BOB PREDMORE
OBSESSIONS: LIZARDS AND RABBITS
NAUGHTIEST DEED: HAVING SELECTIVE HEARING
KNOWN ACCOMPLICES: HER CHILDREN BEBE AND BRIX
FAVORITE PASTIME: CHECKING THE VINES FOR BIRD NESTS

ANNA

BEATRIX AKA **BEBE**

FAVORITE PASTIME: RUNNING
THE SHOW WITH ALL THE TOYS
FAVORITE FOOD: CHICKEN JERKY
OBSESSION: BEING THE LEAD DOG
OWNERS: BARB AND BOB PREDMORE
PET PEEVES: SKUNKS AND STINK BUGS
NAUGHTIEST DEED: BEING A DOMINATING DIVA

OWNER: BRIAN PREDMORE
FAVORITE FOOD: CHICKEN JERKY
PET PEEVES: SKUNKS AND JAVELINA
FAVORITE PASTIME: PLAYING WITH BRIAN
OBSESSION: GETTING ALL THE ATTENTION
NAUGHTIEST DEED: USING THE STATUE
OF ST. FRANCIS AS 'A FIRE HYDRANT'

BRIX

GERMAN SHEPHERDS, 3 | **ALCANTARA VINEYARD AND WINERY** COTTONWOOD, AZ | 123

MONTE

OWNER: RICK BUFFINGTON
NAUGHTIEST DEED: CLIMBING ONTO TABLES
AFTER EATING ALL THE WINE TASTING FOOD SCRAPS
FAVORITE PASTIMES: CHEWING CORKS AND PLAYING WITH MOCHA
PET PEEVE: BEING LOCKED IN HIS KENNEL WHEN IT'S NOT TIME TO SLEEP

COUGAR VINEYARD AND WINERY TEMECULA, CA | LABRADOR, 6 MONTHS

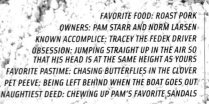

FAVORITE FOOD: ROAST PORK
OWNERS: PAM STARR AND NORM LARSEN
KNOWN ACCOMPLICE: TRACEY THE FEDEX DRIVER
OBSESSION: JUMPING STRAIGHT UP IN THE AIR SO
THAT HIS HEAD IS AT THE SAME HEIGHT AS YOURS
FAVORITE PASTIME: CHASING BUTTERFLIES IN THE CLOVER
PET PEEVE: BEING LEFT BEHIND WHEN THE BOAT GOES OUT
NAUGHTIEST DEED: CHEWING UP PAM'S FAVORITE SANDALS

GRIFFIN

BISMARCK

OWNER: JOHN JORDAN

FAVORITE PASTIME: MANIPULATING
PEOPLE INTO DOING HIS BIDDING

PET PEEVE: WATCHING HUMANS EAT

FAVORITE FOOD: WHATEVER JOHN IS EATING

OBSESSIONS: CATCHING MICE AND WATCHING TV

NAUGHTIEST DEED: BRINGING DEAD MICE HOME

KNOWN ACCOMPLICES: NIMITZ, ROSIE AND THE WINERY STAFF

HARLEY

PET PEEVE: SKUNKS
OBSESSION: DIGGING
FAVORITE TOY: PURPLE ELEPHANT
OWNERS: BRENT AND KATIE YOUNG
NAUGHTIEST DEED: DIGGING UP GRANDMA'S GARDEN
FAVORITE PASTIMES: SUNBATHING AND DREAMING OF DIGGING

FAVORITE TOY: BALL
KNOWN ACCOMPLICE: HARLEY
OWNERS: BRENT AND KATIE YOUNG
OBSESSION: ANYTHING THAT SQUEAKS
FAVORITE PASTIMES: RACING AND CHASING BALLS

TINA

DACHSHUNDS, 4 & 7 | *JORDAN WINERY* HEALDSBURG, CA | 127

FAVORITE TOY: KINDLING
FROM THE WOOD FIRED OVENS

OWNERS: ANDY AND PAIGE WILCOX

FAVORITE FOOD: BREADSTICKS DANGLING
AT EYE LEVEL BY TASTING ROOM VISITORS

NAUGHTIEST DEED: CHASING GREY KITTY AWAY

KNOWN ACCOMPLICES: BERNIE, HEINZ, FLUFFY, OLIVE,
THE CHUCK WAGON (A.K.A. CHARLIE) AND WILE E.

FAVORITE PASTIME: CHASING WILD TURKEYS IN THE VINEYARDS

GUS

LAMBERT BRIDGE WINERY HEALDSBURG, CA | LABRADOR, 5

OWNER: GREG WILCOX
FAVORITE FOOD: LIVERWURST
OBSESSION: CONSTANT AFFECTION
FAVORITE TOY: FLUFFY (14 LB. SHNITZU)
KNOWN ACCOMPLICES: GUS, FLUFFY AND WILE E.
FAVORITE PASTIME: SOLICITING TUMMY RUBS FROM GUESTS
NAUGHTIEST DEED: BEING SLOPPY AROUND HER WATER BOWL

BERNIE

WILE E. WILCOX

OWNER: GREG WILCOX
NAUGHTIEST DEED: RELEASING
A VISITING DOG FROM HIS LEASH
PET PEEVE: HAVING TO GO INSIDE
OBSESSION: TEASING HIS OLDER SISTER BERNIE
FAVORITE FOOD: ANYTHING THE OTHER DOGS ARE EATING
FAVORITE PASTIME: WATCHING THE WORLD GO BY FROM THE WINERY DECK

LAMBERT BRIDGE WINERY HEALDSBURG, CA | GREAT PYRENEES, 9 MONTHS

PET PEEVE: BATHS
FAVORITE TOY: THE CAT
OWNERS: CHRIS AND BRENDA LYNCH
FAVORITE PASTIMES: BOASTING
ABOUT HIS RACING DAYS AND SLEEPING
FAVORITE FOOD: ANYTHING FROM YOUR PLATE
NAUGHTIEST DEED: STEALING FOOD FROM THE PANTRY

PATCH

DOOBIE

PET PEEVE: GETTING A BATH
NAUGHTIEST DEED: SHEDDING
FAVORITE PASTIME: GOING FOR A WALK
FAVORITE TOY: ANY OLD BONE HE FINDS
OWNERS: BILL AND TERESA HINRICHS
OBSESSION: GETTING LOVE FROM EVERYONE
KNOWN ACCOMPLICES: ADAM, ANNA, TANNER AND OLLIE

RANCHITA CANYON VINEYARD SAN MIGUEL, CA | AUSTRALIAN SHEPHERD X, 10

PET PEEVE: PEOPLE
OBSESSION: STARING
FAVORITE TOY: ROPE TOY
FAVORITE PASTIME:
FOLLOWING TERESA AROUND
NAUGHTIEST DEED: EATING TRASH
OWNERS: BILL AND TERESA HINRICHS

TANNER

PET PEEVE: BATHS
OWNERS: VERN AND MAXINE BOLTZ
FAVORITE PASTIMES: EATING AND SLEEPING IN THE SUN
KNOWN ACCOMPLICES: EMME, LITTLE BLUE AND THUNDER
NAUGHTIEST DEED: STEALING CHICKEN TREATS FROM EMME
FAVORITE TOY: HER VERY FIRST TOY EVER – A LITTLE WHITE BEAR

TESS

Yorkville Cellars

SHADOW

PET PEEVE: CLOSED DOORS
FAVORITE TOYS: FIREWOOD
AND BEANIE BABIES
OWNERS: DEBORAH AND EDWARD WALLO
FAVORITE PASTIME: DIVING FOR ROCKS IN THE POND
KNOWN ACCOMPLICES: UPS DRIVERS WHO SNEAK HIM A TREAT
NAUGHTIEST DEED: JUMPING INTO A VISITOR'S CAR AFTER SWIMMING IN THE POND

LILLY

OWNER: SUSAN A. MAHLER
OBSESSION: BEING A MAMMA'S GIRL
FAVORITE TOY: ANYTHING CHLOE HAS
FAVORITE PASTIME: CHASING SQUIRRELS WITH CHLOE
FAVORITE FOOD: FARMSTAND 46 PULLED PORK
NAUGHTIEST DEED: MUDDY PAWS ON THE COUCH

CHLOE

OWNER: SUSAN A. MAHLER
OBSESSION: SWIMMING IN THE POND
FAVORITE PASTIME: RELAXING IN THE HOT
PASO SUN THEN SWIMMING IN THE POND
PET PEEVE: LILLY STEALING HER STUFFED LION
KNOWN ACCOMPLICES: LILLY, BULLIET MAGNUS, BETTY AND BLUE

STAFFORDSHIRE BULL TERRIER X, 3 & MEGA-MUTT, 5 | **CYPHER WINERY** TEMPLETON, CA

SEAMUS

OWNER: JAMIE PETERSON
FAVORITE TOY: MR SQUIRREL
KNOWN ACCOMPLICES: LUKE AND WHITEY
FAVORITE PASTIME: RUNNING AROUND IN CIRCLES
PET PEEVES: BALLOONS, FLAGS AND VACUUM CLEANERS
OBSESSION: HIDING BONES AND CHEW TOYS SO NO ONE CAN STEAL THEM
NAUGHTIEST DEED: STANDING ON HIS HIND LEGS TO STEAL FOOD OFF THE TABLE

PETERSON WINERY HEALDSBURG, CA | POODLE X, 4

OWNER: CHRIS HUEBEL
OBSESSION: RUNNING IN FRONT OF THE
CAR ON THE ROAD LEADING TO THE HOUSE
FAVORITE TOY: OLD DEFLATED SOCCER BALL
FAVORITE PASTIME: GOING FOR RIDES IN THE CAR
FAVORITE FOODS: HARD BOILED EGGS AND PEANUT BUTTER
KNOWN ACCOMPLICES: SEAMUS, BILLY BRUNSON AND ISABELLA
NAUGHTIEST DEED: AN OCCASIONAL RUMMAGE THROUGH THE GARBAGE

LUKE

FAVORITE FOOD: FRESH RAW COUNTRY EGGS
OWNERS: MARCO AND ANN MARIE BORGHESE
FAVORITE PASTIME: RUNNING TO THE TASTING
ROOM WITH MARCO FOLLOWING IN THE CAR
NAUGHTIEST DEED: ROLLING IN YOU KNOW WHAT
PET PEEVES: THE RAIN AND WALKING IN PUDDLES
KNOWN ACCOMPLICE: BOCCE FROM THE HARVEST INN
FAVORITE TOY: "AUSSIE NATURAL" STUFFED RABBIT TOY

BRIX

CASTELLO DI BORGHESE WINERY CUTCHOGUE NY | BRACCO ITALIANO, 7

OBSESSION: DAVID

FAVORITE FOOD: APPLES

OWNER: DAVID MORRISETTE

FAVORITE TOY: PLASTIC MILK JUG

*FAVORITE PASTIMES: CARRYING IN THE
GROCERIES AND BEING AT DAVID'S SIDE*

*NAUGHTIEST DEED: OPENING HOUSE
DOORS TO EAT THE FOOD OFF THE COUNTER*

PET PEEVE: SOMEONE ELSE GIVING DAVID ATTENTION

FAVORITE TOY: STICKS

OWNER: DAVID MORRISETTE

*FAVORITE PASTIMES: EATING AND
GOING TO WORK AT THE WINERY*

*OBSESSIONS: GETTING ATTENTION,
SWIMMING AND DID I MENTION FOOD?*

NAUGHTIEST DEED: GETTING INTO THE GARBAGE

KNOWN ACCOMPLICES: BARNABAS, LUKE AND CAESAR

PET PEEVE: TOO MANY OTHER DOGS COMPETING FOR ATTENTION

LUCKY

"*Talent hits a target no one else can hit;*
Genius hits a target no one else can see."

—— **ARTHUR SCHOPENHAUER**

CANINE CONTEMPLATIONS

by Schopenhauer
(PHILOSOPHER, APHORIST, SCHEMING BEAGLE)

SO I'M SNOOZING UNDERNEATH THE TABLE in the evening and suddenly hear information filtering down into my velvet ears – and I can hardly believe it! She always dresses in jeans or somesuch comfy clothes but now I'm listening to a conversation about smart clothes been worn in palaces and castles, royalty, dukes and duchesses, weddings in Westminster Abbey. Wait, now she's being more expansive. Forget about the tractor I'm always running after – Rolls Royces and chauffeurs, being collected at the bottom of airplane boarding ramps and being whisked away (those must have been the days!) It all sounds glamorous but I wonder if she had the time for important things, like long walks and discovering new smells? It all sounds a bit grand. I wonder if she's drinking too many glasses of wine and is just getting carried away?

Now she's talking about her great-grandfather who discovered some huge rock in the middle of Australia. Very stark and beautiful, she's saying. This sounds more interesting to me. I can imagine that vast space for exploring new and strange smells and having fun chasing kangaroos, although even I would be challenged to keep up with them as they seem to be able to do giant spring-like jumps thanks to that ridiculous non-wagging tail which gives them an unfair advantage. Well, I'll never know as I refuse to spend all those months in quarantine just to satisfy my curiosity – and I have plenty of the latter. So much so that she's made the vineyard escape-proof as when I get tired of chasing the peacocks here, it's fun to get out and about and give all those deer something to think about. And she thinks just because I explore for hours that I might get lost. I honestly think she sometimes forgets that I'm a beagle and that I have this amazing nose so of course I'd know how to find my way home. I just like to have a bit of an adventure now and again – and it certainly sounds as though she's had a few!

I wonder if all these people are leaving soon? All this talking and laughing – and oh no, more wine! I'm going to wander off somewhere quieter now and get some real sleep.

SCHOPENHAUER'S FAITHFUL SCRIBE WAS **ANGELA DOWNER MOENCH** WHO WAS BORN IN AUSTRALIA WHERE SHE STAYED UNTIL HER EARLY TEENS, THEN LIVED IN LONDON AND FOR THE PAST 3 DECADES HAS HAPPILY LIVED IN THE TEXAS HILL COUNTRY WHERE SHE AND HER PHYSICIAN HUSBAND HOWARD HAVE CREATED AND BUILT STONE HOUSE VINEYARD AND WINERY.

SCHOPENHAUER

PET PEEVE: THE WORD "NO"
OBSESSION: DIGGING HOLES
FAVORITE TOY: ANYTHING THAT SQUEAKS
OWNERS: ANGELA AND HOWARD MOENCH
FAVORITE PASTIME: CHASING THE PEACOCKS
KNOWN ACCOMPLICES: MILES, ARCHER, AND TRINITY
NAUGHTIEST DEED: STEALING CRAIG McGILL'S SHOES

STONE HOUSE VINEYARD SPICEWOOD, TX | BEAGLE, 2

KNOWN ACCOMPLICES: THE TWO CATS
OWNERS: DAVID PAGE AND BARBARA SHINN
NAUGHTIEST DEED: ATTACKING MOVING BROOMS
OBSESSION: KEEPING TINY STICKS IN HER
MOUTH AND DEPOSITING THEM ON VISITORS' LAPS
FAVORITE TOYS: FRISBEE AND STOLEN COLLEGIATE BASEBALLS
PET PEEVE: CHICKENS OF ALL TYPES (UNLESS THEY'RE IN HER BOWL)
FAVORITE PASTIME: TRYING TO PLAY STICK AND BALL AT THE SAME TIME

PANDA

LUPO

FAVORITE FOOD: BEEF
FAVORITE TOY: STICKS
OWNER: DARYL SATTUI
KNOWN ACCOMPLICE: YANA
FAVORITE PASTIMES: CHASING STICKS
AND HANGING OUT WITH DARYL
PET PEEVE: BEING LEFT BY HIMSELF

CASTELLO DI AMOROSA CALISTOGA, CA | GERMAN SHEPHERD, 6

FAVORITE TOY: MR. MONKEY
PET PEEVE: GOING ON WALKS
FAVORITE PASTIME: SNUGGLING
OBSESSION: BEING CARRIED AROUND
OWNERS: TRACY AND LINDSAY McARDLE
NAUGHTIEST DEED: TERRORIZING MR. MONKEY

FAVORITE TOY: LEIA
FAVORITE FOOD: BACON
PET PEEVE: OTHER DOGS
OWNERS: TRACY AND LINDSAY McARDLE
OBSESSION: STICKING HIS HEAD OUT OF THE CAR WINDOW
NAUGHTIEST DEED: SUFFERING FROM NAPOLEON COMPLEX

SADIE

OWNER: GENE ESTES
PET PEEVE: THE LARGE TREE LIZARD
FAVORITE TOYS: THE GRANDCHILDREN'S
NAUGHTIEST DEED: HEELING GROUNDSKEEPERS,
POOL CLEANERS AND PEST CONTROLLERS
OBSESSION: CHASING AND BARKING AT SQUIRRELS
FAVORITE PASTIMES: GREETING PEOPLE AND BEING PETTED

LOST OAK WINERY BURLESON, TX | BLUE HEELER X, 7

COCO

FAVORITE TOY: MONKEY
FAVORITE FOOD: ALMONDS
PET PEEVE: VACUUM CLEANER
FAVORITE PASTIME: BUGGING MOXIE
OBSESSION: PLAYING "GET THE KITTY"
OWNERS: MARK CARTER AND SHERRI DOBAY
NAUGHTIEST DEED: ESCAPING OUT OF A TOP
FLOOR WINDOW ONTO THE ROOF OF THE HOUSE

MOXIE

FAVORITE TOY: CHEETAH
FAVORITE FOOD: SALAMI
PET PEEVE: WHEN COCO IS IN HER BED
OBSESSION: KEEPING COCO OUT OF HER BED
OWNERS: MARK CARTER AND SHERRI DOBAY
NAUGHTIEST DEED: OPENING THE UPSTAIRS WINDOW
AND TELLING COCO TO "GO SEE WHAT'S OUT ON THE ROOF"

FAVORITE TOY: CONNOR
KNOWN ACCOMPLICE: JACQUE THE CAT
OWNERS: CHENYN AND JOSIAH JOHNSON
OBSESSION: RIDING IN THE BACK OF THE TRUCK
NAUGHTIEST DEED: SCRATCHING OUT PART OF A WALL
PET PEEVES: GETTING A HAIRCUT AND HAVING HIS TAIL TOUCHED
FAVORITE PASTIME: EATING TACOS ON EMPLOYEE LUNCH BREAKS

BEHR

PRESTON PREMIUM WINES PASCO, WA | LABRADOODLE, 5

PET PEEVE: CATS
OBSESSION: TENNIS BALLS
NAUGHTIEST DEED: SWALLOWING
HALF A BLACK WALNUT SHELL
OWNERS: RAY AND LORI TELDESCHI
FAVORITE FOODS: POPCORN AND BANANAS
FAVORITE TOY: TALLULAH THE BULLMASTIFF
FAVORITE PASTIME: TAKING TALLULAH'S BONES

VITO

DIVA

FAVORITE TOY: MOUSEY TOY
OWNERS: ROD AND CYNTHIA SNAPP
FAVORITE FOOD: GOURMET WET DOG FOOD
NAUGHTIEST DEED: STEALING FOOD FROM
VINNEY AND PUTTING IT IN PEOPLE'S SHOES
FAVORITE PASTIME: LAYING ON ANYONE'S LAP
OBSESSION: STOPPING HER BROTHER VINNEY FROM GETTING ATTENTION

JAVÈLINA LEAP VINEYARD CORNVILLE, AZ | CHINESE CRESTED DOG, 9

VINEYARD AKA VINNEY

OWNERS: ROD AND CYNTHIA SNAPP
FAVORITE TOY: CHEW BONE RAWHIDE
FAVORITE FOOD: ALL THREE POUNDS A DAY
FAVORITE PASTIME: PLAYING WITH HIS SISTER DIVA
OBSESSION: SAYING "LOVE YOU" UNTIL HE GETS HIS COOKIES
NAUGHTIEST DEED: STEALING DIVA'S TREATS WHEN NO ONE IS LOOKING

"*Acquiring a dog may be the only opportunity*
a human ever has to choose a relative."

—— MORDECAI WYATT JOHNSON

NINER
WINE ESTATES

BELLA

OWNER: ALLI ADDISON
PET PEEVE: TAKING BATHS
FAVORITE TOYS: DRYER SHEETS
FAVORITE FOOD: ANYTHING EDIBLE
NAUGHTIEST DEED: STEALING FOOD ON A DAILY BASIS
FAVORITE PASTIMES: EATING AND RIDING IN THE TRUCK

DUNKEL

PET PEEVES: PUPPIES
AND VEGGIE TREATS
OWNER: LORNA KREUTZ-DUGGAN
FAVORITE TOY: SQUEAKY MONKEY
FAVORITE PASTIME: CHASING LIZARDS
NAUGHTIEST DEED: JUMPING ON THE TABLE
AND EATING ALL BUT ONE OF THE CHICKEN TACOS

KAYLA

OWNER: JASON YEAGER
NAUGHTIEST DEED: FINDING
DEAD ANIMALS TO ROLL ON
FAVORITE FOOD: T-BONE STEAK
OBSESSION: CHASING LASER DOTS
FAVORITE TOY: SQUEAKING DRAGON
FAVORITE PASTIME: RUNNING ON THE BEACH
PET PEEVES: BROOMS AND VACUUM CLEANERS

NINER WINE ESTATES PASO ROBLES, CA | ROTTWEILER X, 6

OWNER: PATRICK MURAN

OBSESSION: GOING TO WORK
AT THE WINERY WITH PATRICK

PET PEEVE: NOT BEING ALLOWED
TO CRAWL UP AND SIT ON LAPS

FAVORITE PASTIME: RUNNING IN
A FIGURE EIGHT IN THE BACKYARD

NAUGHTIEST DEED: DIGGING UP
THE FRESHLY PLANTED LEMON TREE

BELL

FAVORITE PASTIME: CHEWING
THE FACES OFF STUFFED TOYS
OWNER: LISA DISMUKES-BRESSLER
OBSESSIONS: FOOD, TOYS AND SLEEPING
PET PEEVES: SQUIRRELS, CATS AND ANYTHING
ELSE THAT MOVES WITHOUT HER PERMISSION
FAVORITE FOOD: WHATEVER'S ON LISA'S PLATE
FAVORITE TOY: STUFFED CATERPILLAR (WITH NO FACE)

LOLA

MARKHAM VINEYARDS ST. HELENA, CA | CAVALIER KING CHARLES SPANIEL, 5

CLYDE

OWNER: KIMBERLEE NICHOLLS

NAUGHTIEST DEED: BURROWING
OUT OF THE YARD REPEATEDLY

FAVORITE FOOD: IRRIGATION LINES

FAVORITE TOY: SISTER COCO'S COLLARS

PET PEEVES: RULES AND RESTRICTIONS

OBSESSIONS: DESTROYING LANDSCAPING
DECORATIONS AND EATING DECK RAILING

KNOWN ACCOMPLICE: HIS BROTHER TUCKER

TUCKER

OWNER: NICOLE ATKINS

FAVORITE PASTIMES: SWIMMING
IN THE CREEK AND CATCHING FLIES

FAVORITE TOY: PURPLE RUBBER BONE

KNOWN ACCOMPLICE: HIS BROTHER CLYDE

NAUGHTIEST DEED: EATING A BATCH OF
BROWNIES AND A CELL PHONE IN ONE SITTING

PET PEEVE: NOT BEING ALLOWED ON THE BED OR COUCH

OBSESSIONS: USED KLEENEX AND SWEATY UNDERARMS

PEPPER

OWNER: JANET MOSHIN
FAVORITE PASTIME: SNIFFING
PET PEEVE: BEING LEFT ALONE
KNOWN ACCOMPLICE: EVERYONE
OBSESSION: CHASING ANIMALS

MOSHIN VINEYARDS *HEALDSBURG, CA* | *ENTLEBUCHER MOUNTAIN DOG, 11*

FAVORITE FOOD: SAUSAGE
FAVORITE TOYS: THE EVIL GAMECOCK
AND THE GREAT CLEMSON FOOTBALL
NAUGHTIEST DEED: WANDERING OFF
PET PEEVE: SMOKE DETECTORS GOING OFF
FAVORITE PASTIME: ROAMING THE VINEYARD
OWNERS: BOYD PEARSON AND GINA HUDSON
OBSESSION: GNAWING ON THE EVIL GAMECOCK
KNOWN ACCOMPLICES: ADA, OLLIE, HENK AND CODY

RASTA BEAUX

SIMON

OWNER: DEBBIE LEHMANN
KNOWN ACCOMPLICE: SHERMAN
FAVORITE PASTIME: FINE DINING
FAVORITE FOOD: SALMON EN CROÛTE
NAUGHTIEST DEED: CATCHING A DUCK
OBSESSION: CHASING DUCKS AROUND THE POND
FAVORITE TOYS: STUFFED ALLIGATOR, HEDGEHOG AND MOOSE

FAVORITE FOOD: CHEESE
FAVORITE TOY: SQUEAKY STUFFED DUCK
NAUGHTIEST DEED: MARKING HIS TERRITORY
OBSESSIONS: CHEESE AND HOLES IN THE DIRT
OWNERS: KIT CRAWFORD AND GARY ERICKSON
KNOWN ACCOMPLICES: LADDIE, COOPER AND CHARLIE
PET PEEVE: WHEN OTHER DOGS INTERRUPT HIS 'ME' TIME
FAVORITE PASTIMES: DIGGING HOLES AND CHASING AFTER LIZARDS

SPARKEY

MAYA

FAVORITE PASTIME: PLAYING FETCH

FAVORITE FOOD: MEAT SNACKS THAT ALEXIS BRINGS HOME FROM WORK

OWNERS: COBEN AND ALEXIS ALEXANDER

PET PEEVE: SOMEONE SITTING IN HER SPOT ON THE COUCH

OBSESSION: DESTROYING THE SEAM ON ANY STUFFED ANIMAL

NAUGHTIEST DEED: GETTING EXCITED AND JUMPING ON GUESTS

BENNETT

OBSESSION: ANYTHING MAYA IS DOING

OWNERS: COBEN AND ALEXIS ALEXANDER

FAVORITE FOOD: ANYTHING MAYA IS EATING

FAVORITE TOY: ANY TOY MAYA IS PLAYING WITH

FAVORITE PASTIME: WRESTLING WITH BIG SISTER MAYA

PET PEEVE: WHEN MAYA WANTS TO RELAX AND WON'T PLAY

NAUGHTIEST DEED: CHASING AND ANNOYING THE TWO CATS

FAVORITE FOOD: CHEESE
OWNER: SUSAN MARTINI
PET PEEVE: BEING TOLD "NO"
OBSESSION: TAKING UNDERWEAR AND
SOCKS FROM THE WASHING MACHINE
NAUGHTIEST DEED: UNPLUGGING THE PHOTOCOPIER
THEN CHEWING THROUGH THE POWER CORD
KNOWN ACCOMPLICES: FINNEGAN AND KELLY

DOOLEY

HENRY

OWNER: JOHN TEVIS
FAVORITE PASTIME: GOING TO THE BEACH
KNOWN ACCOMPLICE: BUDDY THE BEAGLE
NAUGHTIEST DEEDS: SLEEPING ON TASTING
ROOM MERCHANDISE AND EATING CAT FOOD
OBSESSION: CUSTOMERS WITH PICNIC LUNCHES
FAVORITE FOODS: CAT FOOD, TRI-TIP AND GREENIES

HARRIET THE AIREDALE TERRIER

by Greg Duncan Powell

YOU DON'T GET TO CHOOSE YOUR FAMILY. This is as it should be. Given free rein most people make terrible decisions so it's a good thing that families are bestowed rather than chosen. That is except for dogs. A dog does not get to choose who he or she goes home with – the decision is all with the flawed human being. Which means, unless you adopt a stray that wanders into your world, you consciously decide the size, look and behaviors of your pooch – a difficult proposition for the indecisive, vacillating and irresolute. It was with this trio of foibles, and after five dogless years that we entered the market for a puppy.

There were a few criteria the puppy had to meet. The kids are young – aged 7, 5 and 2.5 years old so we didn't want a canine that was too toothy. There was also the problem that some dogs made my beloved sneeze. We couldn't quite work out why or which breeds irritated her beautiful nostrils but we think it had something to do with the more 'sheddy' dogs. We have a problem with the local fauna eating our garden and terrorizing the children so if our dog could persuade marauding marsupials to go elsewhere that would be good. From a selfish point of view, I wanted a dog that could handle itself in the surf, and if it could sniff out a wine fault that would be very handy too.

After the checklist was complete, an identikit picture would show a pooch that had no hair, no teeth, webbed feet, a bark that would scare the bejesus out of the swarthiest swamp wallaby and an overdeveloped snout that could detect brettanomyces at fifty paces. If such a breed did exist, it would fail the cute and cuddly test – which is what the kids wanted.

We studied dog breeds and discussed the attributes of labradoodles, caboodles, maltrievers, dalmweilers and plugs and eventually decided we didn't want any of that nonsense. We wanted a traditional dog. A Labrador would be the sensible choice but not particularly exiting, a Jack Russell could be a solution but the thought of all that hyperactivity made me feel tired.

I have a long-standing affection for Staffies after my much-loved Hillary, but getting another one would be wrong – like going out with someone who looked exactly like your ex. Having discussed the merits of Portuguese Waterhounds, Basengis and everything in between, and with the kids poring over the photos in the various volumes of Wine Dogs, *for some inexplicable reason we decided on an Airedale Terrier.*

I'd always liked them. They had a look about them – dignified, full of character – however, my experience with Airedales was zilch. I had never known or even patted an Airedale. I did some research. It wasn't encouraging. They weren't at the top of the intelligence list. In fact, in Stanley Coren's The Intelligence of Dogs, *Airedales occupied 29th spot. But then again I never excelled in IQ tests so who was I to judge a dog? Besides, Border Collies were at the top of the list so that threw the whole thing into disrepute. The Airedale was from Yorkshire and the River Aire where they were bred from a mixture of the Otter Hound and the Welsh Terrier. Known as the 'King of Terriers' (they're the largest), they'd been used for hunting river rats, for carrying messages and finding wounded in the various wars and even as police dogs. They were meant to be pretty good family dogs and were apparently one of the better breeds for sensitive noses.*

Having decided the Airedale was for us, we set about trying to get a pup. Impossible. In Australia, NSW breeders of Airedales were as rare as pretty pugs. The Airedale is no longer a fashionable breed. Its heyday was between 1900 and the Second World War. Some Airedales had gone down with the Titanic *and President Roosevelt had a couple in the Oval Office. By 1986 in Australia there were 534 Airedale puppies born and by 2005 they were an endangered species and that figure had dropped to 191. Getting an Airedale puppy was not going to be easy. The search spread wider and wider until we located a breeder in Gippsland in Victoria.*

We paid a deposit and were put in a queue behind five other families awaiting mating, conception and the birth of a female pup. While teaching the kids the virtue of patience, the long wait gave us plenty of time to think up names. Agnes, Nancy, Eleanor, Gladys, Grace, Mabel, Kathleen, Euphemia and Banana were all considered and we had about five names on the short list when one day an email came into the inbox, alerting us to the birth of our pup.

She was the produce of Tjuringa Romper Stomper and Tjuringa Extreme Sport and we waited another agonizing eight weeks until I could drive the 13 hours to Gippsland to collect her. On the long trip back I had plenty of time to get to know her. She was definitely not an Agnes, possibly a Kathleen, maybe even a Sadie. Her pedigree name was Cassie and that seemed to suit but the family was on the phone. She was Harriet, and I was not allowed to call her anything else!

When I finally got Harriet home, the kids were so excited they freaked her out and she hid under the couch. But not for long, revenge came quickly with her needle-sharp puppy teeth and their soft skin and treasured toys.

An eight-week old puppy is like having a baby that doesn't wear nappies and has very sharp teeth. They cry, poo and wee everywhere, get into everything and destroy the most precious things. They are a curse in an open-plan house. We had baby-proofed our place but it was impossible to dog-proof it, and it wasn't long before Harriet and I were banished to the spare room.

As I write, Harriet is four and a half months of age, the marriage has survived, most of the house is intact and she's turning into a pretty good dog. She sleeps outside without whinging and has the toilet training sorted. As far as the original checklist goes, she's ticking a few boxes. She sometimes plays a bit rough with the kids – but so do they, she doesn't make my beloved sneeze, she is a champion marsupial chaser, and she is very cute and when sleepy quite cuddly. The wine skills are coming along nicely too. While she is not yet what I would call a 'Wine Dog', she has been paying close attention during tastings and helping with any spillages – particularly if it's expensive cabernet sauvignon.

AUSTRALIAN **GREG DUNCAN POWELL** HAS BEEN WRITING ABOUT WINE AND OTHER DRINKS FOR MOST OF HIS ADULT LIFE. CURRENTLY HE IS DRINKS EDITOR FOR 'MASTERCHEF', PLAYING GUITAR WITH 'THE SWINGING GONADS' AND WRITING LOADS OF BOOKS. HIS MOST RECENT WORKS ARE *BEER – A GAUGE FOR ENTHUSIASTS* (MURDOCH BOOKS) AND *GLOVEBOX GUIDE TO WINE TOURING*. WWW.GREGDUNCANPOWELL.COM.AU

MAMBO

PET PEEVE: OLIVES
FAVORITE FOOD: RADISHES
OWNERS: TOM AND JODIE DAUGHTERS
FAVORITE TOY: PURPLE STUFFED ANIMAL
FAVORITE PASTIME: SLEEPING NEAR JODIE
KNOWN ACCOMPLICE: THE WATSON FAMILY

FAVORITE FOOD: DOG FOOD
OWNERS: TOM AND JODIE DAUGHTERS
FAVORITE TOYS: HIS RHINO AND HIS LOVEY
FAVORITE PASTIME: MEETING NEW FRIENDS
NAUGHTIEST DEED: SNEAKING SOCKS AND SHOES
OBSESSION: THINKING THE WATER BOWL IS HIS TOY
KNOWN ACCOMPLICES: TOMMY WATSON JR. AND JACK STOWE

RYDER

JAKE

FAVORITE TOY: WINE BARREL BUNG
OBSESSION: NIBBLING ALBERT THE CAT
NAUGHTIEST DEED: CRAWLING INTO BED
AND PUTTING HIS HEAD ON MARK'S PILLOW
PET PEEVE: BARKING AT BILLY FOR TREATS
OWNERS: MARK AND TRACY BURNINGHAM
FAVORITE PASTIME: LUNCHTIME AT THE WINERY
KNOWN ACCOMPLICES: KYA, CHASE AND ALBERT THE CAT

OBSESSION: FOOD
OWNER: NATE REYNES
FAVORITE TOY: PILLOWS
PET PEEVE: OTHER DOGS
FAVORITE FOOD: CARROTS
FAVORITE PASTIME: SITTING IN CARS
NAUGHTIEST DEED: TIPPING GARBAGE CANS
KNOWN ACCOMPLICE: TWO-YEAR-OLD WYATT

GOOBER III

FAVORITE FOOD: TUNA
FAVORITE TOY: SUPER CHICKEN
OBSESSION: GETTING ATTENTION
OWNERS: CINDY AND RANDY GOODMAN
FAVORITE PASTIME: WATCHING THE WOOLLY WEEDERS WORK
PET PEEVE: PEOPLE TOUCHING HER FACE WHILE SHE'S BEGGING
NAUGHTIEST DEED: CHEWING CINDY'S GLASSES FROM THE COFFEE TABLE

KYA

BENZIGER FAMILY WINERY GLEN ELLEN, CA | BERNESE MOUNTAIN DOG, 2

STELLA

OWNERS: THE JONES FAMILY
NAUGHTIEST DEED: TAKING DELICIOUS FOOD FROM CHILDREN'S HANDS
FAVORITE FOOD: YELLOW AMERICAN CHEESE
PET PEEVE: NOT GETTING ENOUGH ATTENTION
OBSESSION: TAKING CARE OF BABIES AND CHILDREN

BELLA

FAVORITE FOOD: BACON
OWNERS: THE CABRAL FAMILY
PET PEEVE: AIR COMPRESSORS
NAUGHTIEST DEED: STEALING A WHOLE STEAK FROM THE TASTING ROOM TABLE
OBSESSIONS: FRISBEES, BALLS AND CATS

OWNER: JOE MISTRETTA
PET PEEVE: LOCKED DOORS
FAVORITE FOOD: TABLE SCRAPS
NAUGHTIEST DEED: MAKING A DEPOSIT
IN THE LIVING ROOM ON A RAINY NIGHT
OBSESSION: GRABBING THE CAT BY THE
SCRUFF OF THE NECK AND DRAGGING HER HOME
FAVORITE PASTIME: FIGHTING WITH HER BUDDY TAJ

OWNER: JEANINE MISTRETTA
FAVORITE TOYS: THE FIVE CATS
FAVORITE PASTIME: CLEANING
UP THE LAWN AFTER WEDDINGS
OBSESSION: BEING WITH JEANINE
NAUGHTIEST DEED: NOT GOING
OUTSIDE TO TAKE CARE OF BUSINESS
PET PEEVE: NOT BEING ALLOWED TO GO IN THE CAR

COMIDA

LAGO GIUSEPPE WINERY TEMPLETON, CA │ BORDER COLLIE X, 1 & CHIHUAHUA, 3

OWNER: MIKE AANERUD
PET PEEVE: BEING ON A LEASH
FAVORITE PASTIME: SWIMMING IN THE LAKE
NAUGHTIEST DEED: GETTING INTO THE TRASH
OBSESSION: BARKING AT CIRCLING VULTURES
KNOWN ACCOMPLICES: MIA, COMIDA, LOTTIE AND THE CATS
FAVORITE FOOD: A BOWL OF NUGGETS WITH CHICKEN BROTH

TAJ

BUSTER

OWNER: TOM RODRIGUES
PET PEEVE: WAITING FOR POSIE TO PLAY
OBSESSION: HERDING ANYTHING INCLUDING TOM
FAVORITE PASTIME: PLAYING WITH HIS SISTER POSIE
NAUGHTIEST DEED: ROLLING IN HORSE, PIG OR COW POOP
KNOWN ACCOMPLICES: POSIE, DOZER, CALI AND OBIE

POSIE

OWNER: TOM RODRIGUES
FAVORITE TOY: WHATEVER BUSTER HAS
FAVORITE PASTIME: CHASING BUTTERFLIES
PET PEEVE: NOT GOING ON A RIDE WITH TOM
OBSESSION: HERDING ANYTHING INCLUDING TOM
NAUGHTIEST DEED: ROLLING IN HORSE, PIG OR COW POOP

PET PEEVE: OTIS THE PUG
FAVORITE TOY: OTIS THE PUG
FAVORITE FOOD: ROAST BEEF
FAVORITE PASTIME: DANCING
OWNERS: THE MANNING FAMILY
OBSESSION: THE RACCOON OUTSIDE
NAUGHTIEST DEED: CHASING SQUIRRELS
DOWN THE HILL AND UP THE TREES

LILY

CODY

FAVORITE TOY: HER BONE
OWNER: ANNETTE BERGEVIN
NAUGHTIEST DEED: CHEWING THE NOSES OFF
ANNETTE'S DAUGHTER'S STUFFED ANIMALS
FAVORITE PASTIME: RUNNING IN THE VINEYARD
OBSESSIONS: A MORNING BLOW DRY AND BEING SUNG TO

BERGEVIN LANE VINEYARDS WALLA WALLA, WA | GERMAN SHEPHERD X, 3

OWNER: FLORENCIA PALMAZ
KNOWN ACCOMPLICE: MAX, THE WINERY CAT
FAVORITE PASTIME: WATCHING OTHERS WORK
PET PEEVE: COLD WET GRASS IN THE MORNING
NAUGHTIEST DEED: TOOTING IN THE TASTING ROOM
FAVORITE FOOD: WHATEVER YOU ARE ABOUT TO EAT

PETRA

JUSTICE

OWNERS: BRIAN
AND SHARON ROEDER

PET PEEVE: AN EMPTY BOWL

FAVORITE PASTIME: STANDING
FACE-FIRST INTO A DRIVING RAIN

FAVORITE TOY: CHUCK-IT STICK

NAUGHTIEST DEED: GETTING DRUNK
ON MOULDY STRAWBERRIES

PEANUT

OWNERS: BRIAN
AND SHARON ROEDER

OBSESSION: WINNING

KNOWN ACCOMPLICES:
ANYONE WHO'LL LISTEN

NAUGHTIEST DEED:
TUNNELING UNDER THE FENCE

FAVORITE PASTIME: BOSSING EVERYONE

BARLEY

OWNERS: BRIAN
AND SHARON ROEDER

FAVORITE PASTIME:
WATCHING SUNSETS

PET PEEVE: YOUR
HEAD ON "HIS" PILLOW

FAVORITE FOOD:
ANYTHING HAND-FED

OBSESSION: STEALING SOCKS

182 **BARREL OAK WINERY** DELAPLANE, VA | GOLDEN RETRIEVER, 4, AMERICAN BULLDOG X, 2 & GOLDEN RETRIEVER, 7

OBSESSION: FETCH
FAVORITE TOY: ROCKS (FOR FETCH)
FAVORITE FOOD: ARTISANAL CHEESE
OWNERS: BRIAN AND SHARON ROEDER
KNOWN ACCOMPLICE: ANYONE WITH CHEESE
NAUGHTIEST DEED: SLURPING WINE OFF THE FLOOR
PET PEEVE: STAFF MEETINGS THAT SPILL OVER INTO FETCH TIME

BIRCH

SAKE

KNOWN ACCOMPLICE: BOUZY
PET PEEVE: GETTING NO ATTENTION
OWNERS: FRED AND JUELLE FISHER
FAVORITE PASTIME: MEETING PEOPLE
NAUGHTIEST DEED: 'GOOSING' ARRIVING GUESTS

FISHER VINEYARDS SANTA ROSA, CA | AKITA, 3

PET PEEVE: CATS
OWNER: LORI STEVENS
NAUGHTIEST DEED: OVERDOSING ON CHOCOLATE
FAVORITE TOYS: LEATHER HANDBAGS AND SHOES
FAVORITE PASTIMES: WALKING IN THE VINEYARD
AND EATING CRUMBS OFF THE TASTING ROOM FLOOR
FAVORITE FOOD: McDONALDS VANILLA ICE CREAM CONES

JAX

AUSTRALIAN SHEPHERD X, 5 | **AIRFIELD ESTATES** PROSSER, WA | 185

BELLA

OWNER: *LORI GROSSNICKLE*
FAVORITE TOY: *PLUSH ANGRY BIRD*
OBSESSION: *BRINGING HOME CRITTERS*
FAVORITE PASTIMES: *CHASING CHIPMUNKS*
NAUGHTIEST DEED: *STEALING THE BUILDERS'*
LUNCHES AND BURYING THEM IN THE WOODS
PET PEEVE: *NOT BEING THE CENTER OF ATTENTION*

OWNER: LORI GROSSNICKLE
FAVORITE PASTIME: BEING
THE OFFICIAL WINERY GREETER
FAVORITE TOYS: PLUSH CHICKEN AND FROG
PET PEEVE: NOT GETTING THE TREATS FIRST
NAUGHTIEST DEED: STEALING FOOD FROM PURSES

OBSESSION: BEING PETTED
OWNER: LORI GROSSNICKLE
PET PEEVE: NOT GETTING PETTED
FAVORITE PASTIMES: SWIMMING AND
WEARING HER LIFE JACKET ON THE BOAT
FAVORITE TOY: JIGGLING BLUE PLUSH BALL

OBSESSION: FLIES
PET PEEVE: RAINY DAYS
NAUGHTIEST DEED: SOILING
THE TASTING ROOM RUG
FAVORITE FOOD: FRENCH BAGUETTE
OWNERS: ANDREW AND DEANNA DICKSON
FAVORITE PASTIME: CRUISING THE DOG PARK
KNOWN ACCOMPLICES: AUNT CASSIE AND COUSIN MOLLY

GUS

ANDREW LANE WINERY ST. HELENA, CA | LABRADOR X, 4

GUS I AM

by Drew Dickson

YOU COULD SAY HE WAS BORN UNDER A LUCKY STAR, but he wasn't... he was born under a porch in Paradise, California. We discovered him, lost and malnourished, during the 4th of July weekend. What were we going to name this new arrival? Sure, he was lucky, but we didn't want to name him that, so we decided to go with plain old 'Gus.'

One advantage of having such a brief, no-nonsense moniker is that the possibilities for nicknames are endless. And over the years, we have developed one for every season, occasion and episode of Gus's life.

Gus: aka 'Haggus', 'Gustoph Chompski', 'Gooseberry', 'Gussy-Up', 'The Gusser', 'Out-of-Gus', 'Royal Goose Man', 'The Gusinator', 'Goose', and 'Bear'. The last one stuck well beyond his puppy years because my wife Deanna loves to ride me for believing Labradors are somehow related to bears. A theory I have, based on the shape of their nose.

The handle 'Gooseberry' arrived during one of our blending sessions; a penchant for outdoor sports involving a gaggle of wintering snow geese begot the name 'Goose'; and he was titled 'Gussy-Up' because he makes us look good.

'The Gusser' was coined once we realized the young lad was responsible for a 20% increase in wine sales upon his move to the winery – "Rack one up for the Gusser!" But it wasn't long before he was banished to the vineyard for soiling the tasting room carpet. That carpet was deemed to have been 'Gusinatored!'

While he played well with all the gentleman farmers, his stoic, vineyard trot looked more like a prance as he refused to touch wet grass with his paws. Hence the moniker, 'The Royal Goose Man'.

At the end of the day, it really doesn't matter what you call him – Gus doesn't mind. He will be what he will be – living life with Gusto!

DREW DICKSON, OWNER AND WINEMAKER OF ANDREW LANE WINERY, NAPA VALLEY CA, HAS BEEN BRINGING INKY PURPLE LOVE TO TOWN SINCE 1978 AND WAS THE CO-AUTHOR OF THE ENVIRONMENTAL GRANT WHICH SECURED THE ONLY RIPARIAN BLOCK ON THE NAPA RIVER AT THE OXBOW.

SADIE

OWNER: BRIAN HARLAN
FAVORITE FOOD: BACON
OBSESSION: CHLOE THE CAT
FAVORITE TOY: STUFFED RABBIT
NAUGHTIEST DEED: SLEEPING IN THE BED
PET PEEVE: THE CAT BEING JUST OUT OF REACH
FAVORITE PASTIME: PLAYING WITH STUFFED ANIMALS

BRIAN ARDEN WINES CALISTOGA, CA | GOLDEN RETRIEVER, 6 MONTHS

CYNNABEAR

OWNERS: THOMAS
AND TAMMY SMALL
(CULTIVE CELLARS)

FAVORITE TOY: BUBBLES

OBSESSIONS: GETTING
ATTENTION AND PLAYING

PET PEEVE: BEDROOM
DOORS BEING CLOSED

KNOWN ACCOMPLICE:
SAMMIE THE CROSS-EYED CAT

ASTRID

OWNER: CHRIS BAKER
(ANCIENT CELLARS)

PET PEEVE: SIRENS

FAVORITE TOY: FISH

NAUGHTIEST DEED: CLEARING
THE KITCHEN COUNTERS

FAVORITE PASTIMES: SWIMMING,
AND PLAYING IN THE SNOW

OBSESSIONS: CAR RIDES AND CHRIS

COCO PUFF

OWNERS: THOMAS
AND TAMMY SMALL
(CULTIVE CELLARS)

NAUGHTIEST DEED: EATING
HOT DOGS OFF THE TABLE

FAVORITE PASTIMES:
SWIMMING AND SUNBATHING

FAVORITE FOODS: RIBS,
FRENCH FRIES AND ICE CREAM

PET PEEVE: BEING LEFT AT HOME

OSO

OWNER: CAMERON VAWTER
FAVORITE TOY: TEDDY BEARS
PET PEEVE: THE "STAY" COMMAND
OBSESSION: HERDING EVERYTHING
FAVORITE PASTIME: WAITING FOR THE UPS TRUCK
NAUGHTIEST DEED: STEALING CARROTS FROM THE HORSES

OWNER: JAE M. CHUN
FAVORITE TOY: BIG LOGS
PET PEEVE: RATTLESNAKES
FAVORITE FOOD: KOREAN SHORT RIBS
NAUGHTIEST DEED: STEALING CAT FOOD
OBSESSION: HAVING SOMETHING TO CARRY IN HIS MOUTH

KAHN

DANA ESTATES ST. HELENA, CA | AUSTRALIAN SHEPHERD, 4 & LABRADOR, 3

ONE-DOG NIGHT

by Benjamin Spencer

MY WIFE AND I MET BLU – a bulldog-heeler mix – at the SPCA in 2008. Blu was two years old and a hard case, according to his records, but we both saw something special in his big brown eyes. It was love at first sight, really. I fell for Blu … much the same way I fell for wine.

To Blu, life in Carmel Valley is a kind of paradise. He enjoys chasing butterflies, napping, and learning tricks (for cookies). In many ways, like me, he settled quickly and comfortably into the perfect gig.

When we adopted Blu, I was staging as a sommelier, plus launching my own wine project, in addition to managing the winemaking at Bernardus. I was very busy and, like many of the normalized things in my life, Blu blended in to the mix. Spring became summer and eventually we settled into the long days of harvest.

Our home is on the Bernardus property, so it's not rare that I'm the first one in or the last one to leave the winery.

One night in October, after a long day of pressing, racking, pump overs, and barrel work, I decided that the (four-hour) late 20-ton delivery of chardonnay could wait until morning to be processed.

I sent the crew home and unloaded the truck myself. I checked the weather report and went home to sleep for a few hours.

As I settled in and closed my eyes, it started raining. With only a ten percent chance of showers, according to the local weather experts, I opted to leave the chardonnay out under the stars.

I had to go back.

Blu came with me.

I unrolled the giant tarp as the mist and wind picked up. Blu watched from the crush pad while I carefully balanced on the spines of the bins, covering the grapes.

Every step was slippery and wet. I was having a rough time of it. It was really coming down.

The tarp grew impossibly heavy with rain water, but I managed to secure it as the sky opened up.

The rain arrived in gusts. There was no time for us to get back to the house. No time to get into the winery. We had to seek shelter immediately.

I lifted one corner of the tarp and crouched under. I convinced Blu to join me. He was wet and scared.

For several long minutes, the rain and wind were relentless.

I commented, "Ten percent chance of rain, huh? I can't remember the last time I saw a storm like this."

Blu looked at me, tentatively. He was shivering.

I was shivering too. I put my arm around him and said, "Weathermen!"

Blu put his head on my shoulder and we waited out the rest of the storm together.

BEN SPENCER IS A WINEMAKER AND WRITER. HE HOLDS A DIPLOMA FROM THE WINE & SPIRIT EDUCATION TRUST AND ANOTHER IN WRITING FROM THE JACK KEROUAC SCHOOL OF DISEMBODIED POETICS. HE IS THE ASSISTANT WINEMAKER AT BERNARDUS WINERY AND THE WINEMAKER/OWNER OF LEOJAMI — BOTH PROJECTS BASED IN CARMEL VALLEY, CALIFORNIA. BEN'S ARTICLES HAVE APPEARED IN BARFLY, MUTINEER, CADILLACCICATRIX AND AT INTOWINE.COM. BEN IS THE EXECUTIVE EDITOR AT WWW.AMERICANWINEWRITER.COM. HIS DOG BLU IS ADJUSTING WELL TO LIFE IN CARMEL VALLEY. BLU'S TALENTS INCLUDE HIGH-FIVES, HUGS, PLAYING CATCH (WITH COOKIES), CHASING BUTTERFLIES, AND HERDING CATS. BLU TURNED SIX IN MAY 2012.

BAILEY

PET PEEVE: HER TOYS
BEING REARRANGED

FAVORITE TOY: DUKE

OWNER: LESLIE RENAUD

OBSESSION: SMELLING THINGS

FAVORITE PASTIME: GARDENING

DUKE

OWNER: LESLIE RENAUD

FAVORITE TOY: BAILEY

NAUGHTIEST DEED: EATING
THROUGH TWO MATTRESSES

FAVORITE PASTIME: SWIMMING

HENRY

FAVORITE PASTIME:
GOPHER HUNTING

NAUGHTIEST DEED:
IGNORING HIS HUMANS

OWNER: AMY FREEMAN

OBSESSION: SWIMMING

PET PEEVE: BEING LEFT AT HOME

OBSESSION: HER BALL
OWNER: MICHAEL FALTZ
FAVORITE TOY: HER BALL
PET PEEVE: MEAN PEOPLE
FAVORITE PASTIME: PLAYING OUTSIDE
KNOWN ACCOMPLICES: BAILEY AND MAYA
NAUGHTIEST DEED: PICKING ON LITTLE DOGS

FAVORITE FOOD: SALAMI
OWNER: GIO MARTORANA
KNOWN ACCOMPLICES: MANDY,
SUSHI, RIVER, LOUISE, BOB, BRODY
AND KITTY (REST HER SOUL)
FAVORITE PASTIME: SQUIRREL HUNTING
NAUGHTIEST DEED: EATING
NONI'S GENOA TO SAN FRANCISCO
SHIP TICKET FROM THE 1920'S
FAVORITE TOY: SOCKS

SUNNY

FIGEAC

NAUGHTIEST DEED: STEALING
FOOD FROM CORINNA THE BABY

FAVORITE PASTIMES: NAPPING
AND DIGESTING HIS T-BONE STEAKS

PET PEEVES: GETTING HIS NAILS
CLIPPED AND CONSTRUCTION NOISES

OBSESSION: BARKING AT THE MAIL MAN

OWNERS: RENÉ AND LAURENCE SCHLATTER

FAVORITE FOODS: T-BONE STEAK AND FRENCH BAGUETTE

VOODOO

OBSESSION: HIS SHADOW

PET PEEVE: BEING LEFT BEHIND

FAVORITE FOOD: ITALIAN SALAMI

OWNERS: RENÉ AND LAURENCE SCHLATTER

FAVORITE TOYS: CORINNA'S STUFFED ANIMALS

FAVORITE PASTIME: BARKING AT BIRDS IN THE SKY

NAUGHTIEST DEED: HIDING BONES UNDER THE PILLOWS

MERRYVALE VINEYARDS ST. HELENA, CA | NEWFOUNDLAND X, 13 & LABRADOR X, 4

FAVORITE TOY: SNAKE
OBSESSION: HIS SHADOW
FAVORITE PASTIME: SPINNING
OWNERS: VICKY AND MICHAEL FARROW
FAVORITE FOOD: IMPORTED AUSTRALIAN BEEF
NAUGHTIEST DEED: RUNNING AWAY FOR 45 MILES
PET PEEVE: NOT BEING TAKEN FOR HIS WALK ON TIME

FAVORITE TOY: TOY SPIDER
PET PEEVE: QUICK MOVEMENTS
OBSESSION: ANYONE NEAR HIS HOUSE
OWNERS: VICKY AND MICHAEL FARROW
FAVORITE PASTIME: RIDING IN THE GATOR
NAUGHTIEST DEED: CLIMBING INTO WINE BARRELS

INSPIRATION VINEYARDS AND WINERY SANTA ROSA, CA | HUSKY X, 2 & ROTTWEILER X, 5

TOBY

NAUGHTIEST DEED:
DESTROYING UNDERWEAR

OBSESSION: RETRIEVING
THINGS THROWN INTO THE POND

FAVORITE FOOD: PEANUT BUTTER

OWNERS: JON AND BARBARA PHILLIPS

PET PEEVE: THE RAIN

OBSESSION: STARING
DOWN GOPHER HOLES

OWNERS: JON AND
BARBARA PHILLIPS

NAUGHTIEST DEED:
STEALING CHEESE AND BREAD
FROM THE NEIGHBORS

ASIA

FAVORITE PASTIME: RUNNING AWAY
PET PEEVES: LOCKDOWN OR THE LEASH
OBSESSIONS: HUNTING RABBITS, CHASING
SQUIRRELS AND PLAYING WITH OTHER DOGS
NAUGHTIEST DEEDS: HITCH-HIKING AND
UNAUTHORIZED SLEEP-OVERS AT THE NEIGHBORS
OWNERS: DEBBIE WAHL AND MICHAEL PEARCE
FAVORITE TOYS: GLOVES AND RUBBER DOG KEYS
FAVORITE FOODS: T-BONE STEAKS AND CAESAR DOG FOOD

DUDLEY

JIGGY PIG

FAVORITE TOYS: BALLS
OWNER: MAX PEPLE-ABRAMS
OBSESSION: BALLS, BALLS, BALLS
FAVORITE PASTIME: CHASING A BALL
KNOWN ACCOMPLICES: BUNNI AND NIKA
FAVORITE FOOD: ANYTHING THAT SMELLS LIKE FOOD
PET PEEVE: HAVING A BALL TAKEN AWAY FROM HIM
NAUGHTIEST DEED: KNOCKING DOWN LITTLE CHILDREN HOLDING A BALL

RUBY

PET PEEVE: BEING STUCK IN THE BACKYARD

FAVORITE PASTIME: SWIMMING IN THE POND ON A HOT DAY

FAVORITE TOY: THE DUMPSTER

OWNERS: JUSTIN NEUFELD AND BROOKE HAMILTON

NAUGHTIEST DEED: MAKING THE GARDEN BED HER PERSONAL BED

CHLOE

FAVORITE FOOD: TILLAMOOK CHEDDAR CHEESE

FAVORITE TOY: ANY STICK

OBSESSIONS: FRISBEES, CHERRIES AND UNCLE NATE

NAUGHTIEST DEED: CONFRONTING SKUNKS THEN SMELLING LIKE THEM

OWNERS: SEAN AND ANNA GILBERT

SYRAH

PET PEEVE: BACKRUBS

FAVORITE PASTIMES: CATCHING FRISBEES AND RELAXING UPSIDE DOWN

NAUGHTIEST DEED: LICKING PEOPLE AT THE WRONG TIME

OBSESSION: ANYTHING THAT MOVES

OWNERS: SEAN AND ANNA GILBERT

FAVORITE TOY: MR. SQUIRREL
FAVORITE PASTIME: CATCHING
CRACKERS AT THE WINERY
FAVORITE FOOD: RIBEYE STEAKS
NAUGHTIEST DEED: EATING A SOFA
PET PEEVE: SHADOW EATING HIS KIBBLES
OWNERS: CHRIS AND SARAH HAMILTON

FAVORITE TOY: HER SNUGGLE
OWNERS: CHRIS AND SARAH HAMILTON
KNOWN ACCOMPLICES: BUBBA AND SARAH
OBSESSION: ROLLING TO SCRATCH HER BACK
PET PEEVE: NOT GETTING ENOUGH SCRATCHES
FAVORITE PASTIMES: SLEEPING ON THE COUCH AND BARKING
NAUGHTIEST DEED: KNOCKING OVER TRASH CANS TO FIND TREATS

CHABLIS

HABU

FAVORITE TOY: BIG BONE
FAVORITE FOOD: BABY RODENTS
OWNERS: NORM AND JANICE ROSENE
FAVORITE PASTIME: WORSHIPPING ARGUS
NAUGHTIEST DEED: CHEWING UP THE
HONDA'S UPHOLSTERY DOWN TO BARE METAL
PET PEEVES: CHIHUAHUAS AND TURKEY VULTURES

KNOWN ACCOMPLICE: ELSA
FAVORITE FOOD: PAPOU'S TOAST
FAVORITE TOY: MR. BILL (PICTURED)
OWNERS: NORM AND JANICE ROSENE
PET PEEVE: FLAPPING TARPS ON TRUCKS
OBSESSION: FINDING BIRD NESTS IN THE VINEYARDS
FAVORITE PASTIME: RIDING WITH JANICE ON THE TRACTOR
NAUGHTIEST DEED: RUNNING AWAY THEN ROLLING IN MANURE

ARGUS

ODYSSEY WINERY CHICO, CA | DOBERMAN PINSCHER, 4 & BERNESE MOUNTAIN DOG, 13

FAVORITE FOODS:
SALAMI AND CHEESE
FAVORITE TOY: BULLY STICKS
OWNERS: VICKI AND CRAIG LEUTHOLD
PET PEEVE: BIG BIRDS IN HIS AIR SPACE
NAUGHTIEST DEED: TEARING DOWN THE
PET-SITTER'S FENCE TO GET OUT OF THE YARD
FAVORITE PASTIME: MOOCHING FROM PICNICKING GUESTS

POTTER

PATTI

OWNER: JIM JUDD
FAVORITE FOOD: FILET MIGNON
NAUGHTIEST DEED: SNORING LOUDLY
PET PEEVE: CARLOADS OF CHIHUAHUAS
OBSESSION: A SOFT PILLOW IN A QUIET CORNER
FAVORITE PASTIME: HAVING SOMEONE RUB HER TUMMY
KNOWN ACCOMPLICES: WINERY STAFF THAT RUB HER TUMMY

J & J CELLARS SAN MIGUEL, CA | BLUE HEELER, 6

FAVORITE TOY: POPPED SOCCER BALLS
OWNERS: MICHAEL AND CAROLYN CHANDLER
OBSESSIONS: CHICKEN AND MEETING PEOPLE
PET PEEVE: CATS DRINKING FROM HIS WATER BOWL
NAUGHTIEST DEED: TAKING CHICKEN OFF THE COUNTER
FAVORITE PASTIMES: GOING FOR WALKS AND CHASING BALLS

BLU

OWNER: NATHALIE VACHÉ
OBSESSION: TENNIS BALLS
FAVORITE FOOD: ROTISSERIE CHICKEN
PET PEEVES: RIDING IN THE CAR AND BATHS
KNOWN ACCOMPLICES: PORTER, KRUZER,
ROSIE, CICCA, GIGI, MILO, DOC AND CRESPO
FAVORITE PASTIME: PLAYING WITH HER TENNIS BALL
NAUGHTIEST DEED: EATING BUSTER'S SOUTHERN BBQ

BISOU

REVANA FAMILY VINEYARD ST. HELENA, CA | LONG-HAIRED DACHSHUND, 7

FAVORITE FOOD: CHICKEN
OWNER: MARGRIT MONDAVI
FAVORITE TOY: A PLUSH MOLE
KNOWN ACCOMPLICE: MARGRIT
PET PEEVES: DARKNESS AND RAIN
FAVORITE PASTIME: PLAYING WITH MALBEC
NAUGHTIEST DEED: DIGGING INTO SHEETS AND PILLOWS

LUCE

OWNER: MICHAEL UYTENGSU
FAVORITE TOY: RUBBER DOUGHNUT
PET PEEVE: HAVING HIS HAIR BLOW-DRIED
FAVORITE PASTIMES: WHEN NOT HUNTING FOR
TRUFFLES, PLAYING FETCH, SWIMMING AND BELLY RUBS
OBSESSIONS: PLAYING BALL AND SCENT TRACKING
FAVORITE FOODS: BISON, GOURMET CHEESE AND TRUFFLES
NAUGHTIEST DEED: FAKING ILLNESS TO GET OUT OF OBEDIENCE CLASS

FINN

TUSK ESTATES OAKVILLE, CA | LAGOTTO ROMAGNOLO, 2

BRODIE

FAVORITE PASTIME: EATING

PET PEEVE: NOT BEING INSIDE THE HOUSE

NAUGHTIEST DEED: KNOCKING OVER THE GARBAGE CANS

OBSESSION: BEING WITH PEOPLE

OWNERS: GLENN AND GAYLE COOK

TANK

FAVORITE FOOD: BONES

FAVORITE TOY: CHEW TOYS

OBSESSION: BEING WITH GLENN AND GAYLE

NAUGHTIEST DEED: RUNNING AWAY FROM THE WINE DOGS PHOTOGRAPHER

OWNERS: GLENN AND GAYLE COOK

WILMA

FAVORITE PASTIME: BEING IN CHARGE

OBSESSION: CONTROL

FAVORITE FOOD: ANYTHING THE OTHER DOGS HAVE

NAUGHTIEST DEED: ESCAPING

PET PEEVE: GETTING UP TOO EARLY

OWNERS: GLENN AND GAYLE COOK

LABRADOR X, 6, ROTTWEILER X, 3 & TIJUANA TICK HOUND, 7 | **COOK FAMILY WINERY** ST. HELENA, CA | 213

SHYLO

PET PEEVE: DIRTY FEET
OWNER: TOBE SHELDON
FAVORITE FOOD: PEA SHELLS
FAVORITE TOY: DYLAN'S SOCKS
OBSESSION: WHERE'S MOMMY? ›
FAVORITE PASTIME: RUNNING AT HIGH SPEEDS
NAUGHTIEST DEEDS: FOOD THEFT AND SOCK DESTRUCTION

SHELDON WINES SANTA ROSA, CA | WEIMARANER, 5

OBSESSION: SQUIRRELS
PET PEEVE: CHIHUAHUAS
OWNER: DYLAN SHELDON
FAVORITE FOOD: ASPARAGUS
FAVORITE PASTIME: MOUNTAIN BIKING
NAUGHTIEST DEED: COUNTER SURFING CHEESE THEFT
FAVORITE TOYS: WINE CORKS AND A STUFFED SQUEAKY DUCK

LUNA

OBSESSION: *THERESA*
FAVORITE FOOD: *CHICKEN*
PET PEEVE: *RUMBLING NOISES*
NAUGHTIEST DEED: *CHEWING A WOODEN CABINET (TO GET TO THE TREATS)*
KNOWN ACCOMPLICE: *SPARKY THE CAT*
OWNERS: *THERESA AND TOM ROCHIOLI*
FAVORITE PASTIME: *CHASING AFTER STICKS*

LULU

RUSTY

FAVORITE PASTIME: GETTING ATTENTION
PET PEEVE: WHEN HIS BROTHERS BUG HIM
OBSESSION: GETTING PETTED
FAVORITE FOOD: ANYTHING HE'S NOT SUPPOSED TO HAVE
OWNER: HOLLY BALANSAG
NAUGHTIEST DEED: STEALING FOOD

ROSIE

FAVORITE FOOD: CHEESE
FAVORITE PASTIME: GREETING WINERY CUSTOMERS
FAVORITE TOY: STUFFED TEDDY
NAUGHTIEST DEED: TAKING CHAPSTICKS OUT OF PURSES
KNOWN ACCOMPLICES: WINSTON, SCOOTER, OLIVER AND TOBY
OWNERS: NORM AND ALICE MOFFATT

ELLI

OWNER: MEGAN BLAKE
FAVORITE PASTIME: CHASING SANDHILL CRANES
FAVORITE FOOD: VENISON
NAUGHTIEST DEEDS: CHASING SANDHILL CRANES
KNOWN ACCOMPLICE: HER AUNT WEEZIE, THE BOSTON TERRIER

GAUGE

OWNER: BRENDAN ROCHE
PET PEEVE: SHORT WALKS
OBSESSION: PLAYING CATCH
FAVORITE TOY: STUFFED DUCKIE
KNOWN ACCOMPLICE: HIS BROTHER TULE
FAVORITE PASTIMES: DUCK HUNTING AND SNUGGLING
NAUGHTIEST DEED: STEALING BRENDAN'S GUINNESS SLIPPERS

FAVORITE TOY: TENNIS BALL

OBSESSION: TUG OF WAR (ALWAYS WINS)

OWNERS: STEVE AND VALERIE ANDREWS

NAUGHTIEST DEED: HELPING HIS
BROTHER BUDDY CHEW UP EIGHT DOG BEDS

PET PEEVE: BUDDY GETTING ALL THE ATTENTION

FAVORITE PASTIMES: SLEEPING
AND LICKING THE CARPET

PET PEEVE: LAWNMOWERS

NAUGHTIEST DEED: CHEWING
UP TWO ANTIQUE CUSHIONS

FAVORITE PASTIMES: CHASING
BIRDS AND TAKING A SHOWER

OBSESSION: CHEWING UP DOG BEDS

OWNERS: STEVE AND VALERIE ANDREWS

FAVORITE TOY: AN UNSTUFFED SQUEAKY SANTA

RYLEY

OWNERS: JOHN AND KELLY JACKSON

FAVORITE PASTIME: HANGING OUT
IN THE KITCHEN AS SOUS-CHEF

OBSESSION: CHASING HOT AIR
BALLOONS THAT INVADE HIS VINEYARD

PET PEEVE: BEING TACKLED
BY HIS BROTHER WOLFI

NAUGHTIEST DEED: HIDING IN VINES

BREE

FAVORITE PASTIME:
WORKING THE VINEYARDS

NAUGHTIEST DEED: CHASING
THE UPS AND FEDEX TRUCKS

OWNERS: BRAD AND KRISTA FOSTER

PET PEEVE: HAVING TO COME INTO THE
WINERY WHEN CALLED

KNOWN ACCOMPLICE: GINGER THE CAT

WOLFI

PET PEEVE: FLYING INSECTS

FAVORITE PASTIME: PLAYING RING-
AROUND-THE-ROSIE ON THE DECK

OBSESSION: TUGGING ON PACKAGES,
PURSES AND GROCERY BAGS

NAUGHTIEST DEED: QUIETLY
NIBBLING HOLES IN LOOSE CLOTHING

OWNERS: JOHN AND KELLY JACKSON

NORTH MOUNTAIN VINEYARD MAURERTOWN, VA | BELGIAN SHEEPDOG, 3, WALKER HOUND, 4 & BELGIAN SHEEPDOG, 3

OWNER: *PINDAR DAMIANOS*
KNOWN ACCOMPLICE: *ANDREW*
FAVORITE TOY: *ANYTHING STUFFED*
FAVORITE PASTIMES: *RUNNING THROUGH THE VINES AND CHASING BIRDS*
FAVORITE FOOD: *ANYTHING HE CAN'T HAVE*
NAUGHTIEST DEED: *TAKING TOYS FROM ANDREW*
OBSESSION: *SITTING ON PINDAR'S LAP WHENEVER POSSIBLE*

JAKE

NAUGHTIEST DEED: BARKING
OWNERS: BOB AND CARLENE RUE
OBSESSION: CHEWING HIS BLANKET
FAVORITE TOYS: BLANKET AND GREEN BALL
KNOWN ACCOMPLICES: WAYMAN AND ROSCO
PET PEEVE: WINERY FRIENDS WITH NO TREATS
FAVORITE PASTIME: FINDING DOG TREATS IN HIS GREEN BALL

ROBERT RUE VINEYARD AND WINERY *FULTON, CA* | DACHSHUND, 5

FAVORITE TOY: CROCOBOB
PET PEEVE: BEING TOLD TO SIT
OWNERS: TRENT AND MARION GHIRINGHELLI
FAVORITE PASTIME: SWIMMING IN THE LAKES
OBSESSIONS: COW POOP AND REARRANGING THE WOOD PILE
NAUGHTIEST DEED: CHEWING OFF THE TRAILER'S LIGHTS AND WIRING

CHACHI

LABRADOR, 6 MONTHS | **HEIBEL RANCH VINEYARDS** ST. HELENA, CA

OWNERS: KATHLEEN AND BOB DELF
NAUGHTIEST DEED: ABUSING HIS 'MINI-ME'
FAVORITE TOYS: HIS 'MINI-ME' AND FLAMINGO
FAVORITE FOODS: CHEESE, FILET, ANY HUMAN FOOD
KNOWN ACCOMPLICES: PRECIOUS, ERNIE, HAILEY AND CHAUNCY
OBSESSIONS: BONES, KATHLEEN AND RIDING SHOTGUN IN THE CAR

MACK

PET PEEVE: BATHTIME
FAVORITE FOOD: BANANAS
OBSESSION: CLEANING HIS FEET
FAVORITE TOYS: TOYS WITH STUFFING
KNOWN ACCOMPLICES: BELLA AND XOCO
NAUGHTIEST DEED: EATING 9LBS OF CAT FOOD
FAVORITE PASTIME: GREETING WINERY VISITORS
OWNERS: COURTNEY HARRIS AND SCOTT CUNNINGHAM

XOCO

OWNER: HALLIE OTEIZA
FAVORITE FOOD: PEANUT BUTTER
OBSESSIONS: SQUIRRELS AND STICKS
KNOWN ACCOMPLICES: MACK AND THE SHEEP
FAVORITE PASTIMES: RUNNING AND CHEWING BONES
PET PEEVE: HER OWNER NOT GETTING UP EARLY ENOUGH
NAUGHTIEST DEED: EATING HER GRANDMA'S THROW PILLOWS

TONKA

PET PEEVE: BATHS
OWNER: DR. GORDON DUTT
FAVORITE PASTIME: HANGING
OUT WITH THE VINEYARD STAFF
OBSESSION: ROLLING IN DEAD SKUNKS
NAUGHTIEST DEED: ROLLING IN DEAD SKUNKS

SONOITA VINEYARDS ELGIN, AZ | AUSTRALIAN SHEPHERD X

OBSESSION: NAPPING
OWNER: DR. GORDON DUTT
NAUGHTIEST DEED: WALKING
THROUGH THE WINERY FLOWER BEDS
PET PEEVE: CUSTOMERS WHO DON'T FEED HIM
FAVORITE PASTIME: PICNICKING WITH CUSTOMERS
KNOWN ACCOMPLICES: MOST CUSTOMERS AND STAFF

TIGER

RILEY

OBSESSION: JUICY KISSES
PET PEEVE: CHEESE DEFICIENCY
OWNERS: LEAH AND MIKE SMITH
FAVORITE PASTIMES: CHASING SQUIRRELS
IN HIS SLEEP AND CHEWING UP FLIP-FLOPS
FAVORITE TOYS: HIS BONE AND RED BANDANA
FAVORITE FOOD: CHEESE, CHEESE AND MORE CHEESE
KNOWN ACCOMPLICES: MIKE, FLIP THE CAT AND SAUVI B
NAUGHTIEST DEED: STEALING CREDIT CARDS OUT OF WALLETS

SPRING MOUNTAIN VINEYARD ST. HELENA, CA | MINIATURE ENGLISH GOLDENDOODLE, 1

FAVORITE FOOD: FRESH FRUIT
NAUGHTIEST DEED: JUMPING ON PEOPLE
PET PEEVE: ENDING A SESSION OF FETCH
OWNERS: RON AND JACKIE ROSENBRAND
FAVORITE TOYS: HER CATS, SEMILLON AND BOOKER
FAVORITE PASTIMES: GOING ON HIKES AND SWIMMING
KNOWN ACCOMPLICES: HER KIDS, CONNER, COLE AND ALEXI

SAUVI B

MAYSY

PET PEEVE: BUGS

FAVORITE FOOD: ICE CREAM

OWNER: MICHAEL DUNHAM

FAVORITE PASTIME: ESCORTING CUSTOMERS FROM THE PARKING LOT TO THE TASTING ROOM

OBSESSION: SOMEONE THROWING A TENNIS BALL FOR HER

NAUGHTIEST DEED: NOT PLAYING WELL WITH LITTLE DOGS

KONNIE

OWNER: JOANNE DUNHAM

FAVORITE PASTIME: SLEEPING AT JOANNE'S FEET

OBSESSIONS: HUNTING GOPHERS AND PLAYING CATCH

NAUGHTIEST DEED: NIPPING ANKLES AS A PROXIMITY WARNING

PET PEEVES: MISSING OUT ON A CAR TRIP AND MIKE DUNHAM SNEEZING

MUNCH

OWNER: ERIC DUNHAM

FAVORITE FOOD: HAM AND CHEESE CROISSANTS

NAUGHTIEST DEED: BRINGING A FRESHLY CAUGHT GOPHER INTO A PACKED TASTING ROOM

PET PEEVES: LITTLE BOYS AND ERIC PACKING TO LEAVE

FAVORITE PASTIME: FOLLOWING ERIC AROUND, HOPING FOR TREATS

OBSESSION: SQUIRRELS
FAVORITE FOOD: CHEESE
OWNER: ANGELA BRAGANINI
FAVORITE TOY: SQUEAKY TIKI
KNOWN ACCOMPLICE: CANNON
PET PEEVE: HAVING HIS TAIL TOUCHED
FAVORITE PASTIMES: CORVETTE AND GOLF CART RIDES
NAUGHTIEST DEEDS: RUNNING AWAY AND STEALING SOCKS

PATRON

SHIBA INU, 4 | **ST. JULIAN WINE CO.** PAW PAW, MI

PET PEEVES: BATHS AND CATS
OWNERS: TOM AND MARY MORGAN
FAVORITE TOY: A RUBBER CHICKEN
OBSESSION: PLAYING IN THE SNOW
KNOWN ACCOMPLICES: NERO AND GRACE
FAVORITE FOODS: MARROW BONES AND ANYTHING COOKED
WITH TRUFFLES (BLACK PERIGORD OR WHITE TUSCAN)
FAVORITE PASTIME: RIDING IN THE TRUCK WITH HER HEAD OUT THE WINDOW

BRYN

THE LENZ WINERY PECONIC, NY | AIREDALE TERRIER, 7

OBSESSION: BLANKETS
KNOWN ACCOMPLICE: KAELIN
OWNERS: JEROL AND JEFFREY RICKARD-BAILEY
FAVORITE TOY: STUFFED SQUEAKY SOCK MONKEY
NAUGHTIEST DEED: COUNTER SURFING FOR FOOD
PET PEEVE: BEING FORCED TO SIT IN THE BACK SEAT OF THE CAR
FAVORITE FOOD: DUCK AND SWEET POTATO DOG FOOD AND CHEETOS

INDY

BAILEY

OBSESSION: FOOD
PET PEEVE: HAVING NO FOOD
NAUGHTIEST DEED: KILLING A DEER
KNOWN ACCOMPLICE: ANYONE WITH FOOD
OWNERS: DONALD AND MADELYN THIESSEN
FAVORITE PASTIMES: LOOKING FOR FOOD AND SLEEPING

FAVORITE PASTIME: FETCHING
FAVORITE TOY: THE NEWSPAPER
OWNERS: DONALD AND MADELYN THIESSEN
OBSESSIONS: FETCHING AND RIDING IN THE GOLF CART
PET PEEVE: NOT BEING ALLOWED TO RIDE IN THE GOLF CART

BUCK III

STACKED STONE CELLARS PASO ROBLES, CA | GOLDEN RETRIEVERS, 13 & 14

PUCK

FAVORITE FOOD: MEATLOAF
PET PEEVE: BEING LOCKED IN THE
KENNEL AND NOT BEING ABLE TO RUN
OBSESSIONS: RUNNING AND BARKING
OWNERS: DONALD AND MADELYN THIESSEN
FAVORITE PASTIME: GETTING LOVE AND ATTENTION
NAUGHTIEST DEED: KILLING THE NEIGHBOR'S CHICKEN

LUCKY

NAUGHTIEST DEED: GETTING LOST
PET PEEVE: SOMEONE TAKING HIS TOY AWAY
OBSESSION: EMPTY PLASTIC WATER BOTTLES
OWNERS: DONALD AND MADELYN THIESSEN
FAVORITE FOOD: NACHO CHEESE FLAVORED DORITOS
FAVORITE PASTIMES: PLAYING WITH ANYONE AND SWIMMING

OWNER:
BRYAN PAGE
FAVORITE TOY: STINKY TUG-O-WAR ROPE
FAVORITE FOODS: BANANAS AND TOMATOES
KNOWN ACCOMPLICES: ROMEO AND HUDSON
OBSESSIONS: ANYTHING THAT SQUEAKS AND LASER POINTERS
NAUGHTIEST DEED: FARTING LOUD ENOUGH TO MAKE A TRUCK DRIVER BLUSH

PET PEEVE: EARLY MORNINGS
OWNERS: MIKE AND KRISTI BAILES
FAVORITE TOY: SQUEAKY GREEN PIG
KNOWN ACCOMPLICE: WILLIE THE CAT
FAVORITE FOOD: GRANNY SMITH APPLES
NAUGHTIEST DEED: LOCKING GRANDPA OUT
OF HIS TRUCK WHILE IT WAS IN MOTION
FAVORITE PASTIMES: SWIMMING AND FETCHING

REYA

OSO

FAVORITE FOOD: BEEF
OWNER: ESTEBAN LLAMAS
FAVORITE TOYS: OTHER DOGS
PET PEEVE: NOT GETTING ATTENTION
FAVORITE PASTIME: HANGING OUT WITH VINEYARD WORKERS
OBSESSION: CHECKING OUT NEW PEOPLE IN THE VINEYARD

BUSTER

OWNER: STAGECOACH VINEYARD
FAVORITE PASTIME: RIDING AROUND
THE VINEYARD IN PICKUP TRUCKS
FAVORITE FOOD: CANNED DOG FOOD
PET PEEVE: STRANGERS IN THE VINEYARD
OBSESSION: LOVING ALL OF THE WORKERS

238 | **STAGECOACH VINEYARD** NAPA, CA | ROTTWEILER, 4 & GERMAN SHEPHERD, 9

OBSESSION: ETHAN'S TOYS
PET PEEVE: COMING INSIDE
KNOWN ACCOMPLICE: SHADOW
FAVORITE PASTIME: CHASING JORDAN
ON THE ATV THROUGH THE VINEYARD
FAVORITE FOOD: ETHAN'S FLOOR CHEERIOS
OWNERS: JORDAN, JEN AND ETHAN HARRIS
NAUGHTIEST DEED: CHASING A HERD OF DEER

MIA

PET PEEVE: BATHS
FAVORITE TOY: RUBBER FROG
NAUGHTIEST DEED: STEALING A
BURNING LOG OUT OF THE FIREPLACE
AND RUNNING AROUND THE HOUSE WITH IT
OWNERS: ANTHONY AND SUZANNE TRUCHARD
FAVORITE PASTIME: SWIMMING IN THE WATER RESERVOIRS

JACK

TRUCHARD VINEYARDS NAPA, CA | LABRADOR, 2

FAVORITE TOY: SQUIRRELS
OWNERS: STEVE AND KELLEY STYRING
FAVORITE FOOD: SLIGHTLY ROTTEN GOPHER
FAVORITE PASTIME: CHASING LOW-FLYING AIRCRAFT
OBSESSIONS: BIRDS, AIRPLANES AND RIDING IN THE TRUCK
KNOWN ACCOMPLICES: THE TALL BOY, THE BUSY GIRL AND PEARL THE CAT
NAUGHTIEST DEEDS: BEGGING FOR CHEESE AND BEING A POTTY-MOUTH ON TWITTER

MOLLY

COLTEN

OWNER: KEELY REED
FAVORITE FOOD: LETTUCE
FAVORITE PASTIME: LICKING
LOTION OFF CUSTOMERS' LEGS
OBSESSION: RIDING THE FORKLIFT
KNOWN ACCOMPLICE: STINKY AND
ANYONE WITH LOTION ON THEIR LEGS
PET PEEVE: PEOPLE WITH LONG PANTS ON

ASIA

FAVORITE PASTIME:
GREETING CUSTOMERS
FAVORITE FOOD: MILK BONES
NAUGHTIEST DEED: ENJOYING
THE NEIGHBOR'S CHICKENS
OWNERS: CHRISTIE AND DICK REED
OBSESSION: THE MILK BONE DRAWER

STINKY

OWNER: KEELY REED
FAVORITE TOYS: FRISBEE
AND COLTEN'S ANKLES
OBSESSION: BARKING
AND CHASING HIS TAIL
NAUGHTIEST DEED: STEALING
CHICKENS OFF TABLE TOPS
PET PEEVES: CATS AND RACCOONS

OWNER: SIMONE MICHEL
FAVORITE FOOD: PEANUT BUTTER
PET PEEVES: KITTIES AND MEN WITH BEARDS
FAVORITE TOY: WOOD AND ANYTHING CUDDLY
OBSESSION: CHASING RABBITS IN THE VINEYARD
FAVORITE PASTIMES: SLEEPING UNDER SIMONE'S DESK
NAUGHTIEST DEED: EATING TWO SHEETS OF COOKIE DOUGH

LEROY GARFUNKEL

THE FRENCHIE REVOLUTION

by Susan Elliott

LIKE A CLASSIC NAPA CABERNET, Frenchie the French Bulldog is blessed with a solid full body, a good nose and a strong, robust character. So it is only natural that he has been the inspiration and driving force behind Frenchie Winery – the only tasting room designed exclusively for dogs.

Located at Raymond Vineyards in the Napa Valley, the winery opened its doors in May 2012 and is the creation of Frenchie's owner Jean-Charles Boisset. "Frenchie was a gift to my beloved wife," says Boisset, "to ensure that she would always be in the company of a French gentleman. In fact, Frenchie is the perfect French gentleman: he's loyal, charming, always up for an adventure, and he never talks back! His playful, debonair and aristocratic style is reflected in the winery and the wines."

Frenchie's bioDOGnamic vineyard is planted to Bordeaux varieties and the resulting wines are suitably Gallic in nature: the 'Napoleon' Red ("pairs well with a nice long belly rub and a nap"), and the 'Louis XIV' Cabernet Sauvignon ("like Versailles, this cabernet has great structure.")

Like many revolutionaries before him, Frenchie had a dream: no dog should have to stay in a hot car while his/her parents enjoyed themselves tasting wine – all creatures deserve the same pleasures. And so, the Frenchie Winery legend was born.

To ensure that Frenchie's fellow pooches are taken care of when their people choose to visit Raymond Vineyards, his winery offers sheer canine splendour: personal 'dog suites', each with their own specially designed wine barrel dog bed; the 'Gallery of Frenchie' featuring portraits of Frenchie posing as famous historical leaders (including Louis XIV, George Washington and Napoleon); a beautiful 'Barkarrat' chandelier; a special dog-friendly tasting bar, which dispenses water for its guests; and an outdoor play area for more active visitors. The property also includes a tasting bar where two-legged guests can sample Frenchie Wines. The bar is complete with a doggie-cam so that pet lovers can keep an eye on their furry friends while visiting the Raymond Winery main tasting room.

Follow Frenchie's campaign for canine viticultural domination by checking out his videos at FrenchieWinery.com. Talk about a winery that's really gone to the dogs... Vive le Frenchie!

OWNER: JEAN-CHARLES BOISSET
FAVORITE TOY: HIS DAD'S MASERATI
OBSESSIONS: CHEESE AND BELLY RUBS
FAVORITE PASTIMES: NAPPING AND EATING
NAUGHTIEST DEED: DIGGING AND GETTING DIRTY
FAVORITE FOOD: ANYTHING CHEF CORNU PREPARES
PET PEEVE: PEOPLE WHO WALK BY AND DON'T SCRATCH HIS HEAD
KNOWN ACCOMPLICES: HOPPER, BRUTUS, PITA, JORDAN AND LILLIE

FRENCHIE WINERY ST. HELENA, CA | FRENCH BULLDOG, 5

PET PEEVE: *BEING TOLD TO STAY*
FAVORITE PASTIME: *QUAIL HUNTING*
FAVORITE FOOD: *RARE PRIME RIBS*
NAUGHTIEST DEED: *ROLLING IN FILTH*
AND THEN JUMPING INTO SCOTT'S TRUCK
OWNERS: *SCOTT AND KATHLEEN McLEOD*

GUINEA

MAGNUM

FAVORITE TOY: DEER HORN
PET PEEVES: SIRENS AND BEING ALONE
OBSESSION: CHASING FOUR-WHEELERS
OWNERS: PERRY AND CHRISTINE CLARK
FAVORITE FOOD: YUGOSLAVIAN SURPRISE MEAT
NAUGHTIEST DEED: EATING AN ENTIRE BAG OF HALLOWEEN
CANDY THEN LITTERING THE YARD WITH WRAPPERS AFTERWARDS

AMIZETTA WINERY ST. HELENA, CA | LABRADOR, 6

FAVORITE FOOD: LAMB CHOPS
PET PEEVE: MAGNUM RUNNING FREELY
OWNERS: EDDIE CLARK AND JENNY WAGNER
NAUGHTIEST DEED: CHEWING IRRIGATION LINES
FAVORITE TOY: AN UNSTUFFED TUG-OF-WAR SQUIRREL
FAVORITE PASTIME: SUNBATHING IN FRONT OF THE WINERY
OBSESSION: CHASING THE FOUR-WHEELER THROUGH THE VINEYARDS

OSA

CALI

FAVORITE FOOD: LEFTOVERS
OWNERS: HANK AND LINDA WETZEL
FAVORITE PASTIME: POINTING AT QUAIL
NAUGHTIEST DEEDS: ROLLING IN THE
MUD AND DIGGING HOLES IN THE GARDEN
OBSESSIONS: RUNNING AND ATTRACTING BURRS
PET PEEVE: BEING INSIDE WHEN ALL THE ACTION IS OUTSIDE

FAVORITE FOOD: RIB EYE STEAK
NAUGHTIEST DEED: COSTING THE
WINERY $1,000 IN STOLEN BUNGS
FAVORITE PASTIME: DUCK HUNTING
OWNERS: HANK AND LINDA WETZEL
FAVORITE TOY: SILICON BARREL BUNG
OBSESSIONS: RETRIEVING AND HUMAN AFFECTION

MATTIE

FAVORITE TOY: BING
OWNERS: VIC AND KATHI POULOS
FAVORITE FOOD: WINERY CRACKERS
KNOWN ACCOMPLICES: SPANKY AND OLIVE
FAVORITE PASTIME: MEETING AND GREETING
OBSESSION: BALLS AND ANYTHING THAT ROLLS
PET PEEVE: NOT BEING ALLOWED TO CHASE THE CAT
NAUGHTIEST DEED: CHEWING THE TASTING ROOM'S BASEBOARDS

BARRIQUE

RILEY

OWNER: CRIS GAMACHE
FAVORITE FOOD: POTATO CHIPS
FAVORITE PASTIME: CHASING SQUIRRELS
KNOWN ACCOMPLICES: OTIS AND PATCHES
NAUGHTIEST DEED: TAKING ON TWO RACCOONS
OBSESSION: PROTECTING CRIS AND THE GRANDCHILDREN
PET PEEVE: BEING DISTURBED WHILE SLEEPING ON CRIS' BED

GAMACHE VINTNERS PROSSER, WA | YORKSHIRE TERRIER, 5

OBSESSION: HER BALL
FAVORITE FOODS: PIZZA AND STEAK
FAVORITE TOY: DOLLY THE STUFFED LION
OWNERS: ALEXANDER DAMIANOS AND FAMILY
FAVORITE PASTIME: CHEWING EVERYTHING IN THE HOUSE
NAUGHTIEST DEED: RUNNING OFF WITH FOUR-YEAR-OLD EVAN'S TOYS
KNOWN ACCOMPLICES: THE NEIGHBOR'S GOLDEN RETRIEVERS AND EVAN

CEE CEE

BONNY

OWNER: ROBERT FOLEY
FAVORITE TOY: TENNIS BALLS
KNOWN ACCOMPLICES: QUARZ AND FRITZ
PET PEEVE: NOT BEING TAKEN FOR A CAR RIDE
NAUGHTIEST DEED: CHEWING UP A STACK OF BOOKS
OBSESSION: STICKING HER HEAD OUT OF THE CAR WINDOW
FAVORITE PASTIME: ATTEMPTING TO CATCH THE JACK RABBITS

OWNER: WILLIAM "BILL" FOLEY
FAVORITE TOYS: VOLLEYBALL OR STICK
FAVORITE PASTIME: PLACING A STICK IN FRONT
OF PEOPLE AND HOPING THEY WILL THROW IT FOR HIM
PET PEEVE: NOT FINDING ANYONE TO PLAY CATCH WITH HIM
NAUGHTIEST DEED: CONSTANTLY SHOVING A STICK IN YOUR LAP
OBSESSION: TRYING TO FIND SOMEONE TO PLAY CATCH WITH HIM

QUARZ

CHALK HILL ESTATE HEALDSBURG, CA | GERMAN SHEPHERDS, 3

MAUDE

PET PEEVE: BATHS
OBSESSION: CAT FOOD
FAVORITE PASTIME:
CHASING SQUIRRELS
OWNER: RICHARD CARMICHAEL
FAVORITE FOOD: BULLY STICKS
NAUGHTIEST DEED: DEVOURING
A CAKE AND A LOAF OF BREAD
JUST BEFORE A DINNER

REX

FAVORITE TOY: STICKS
NAUGHTIEST DEED:
SHARING HIS SLOBBER
OWNER: TRACEY BERUBE
PET PEEVE: RECEIVING
TOO MUCH ATTENTION
FAVORITE PASTIME: RELAXING
OBSESSION: BEING IN THE CAR

MAGGIE

FAVORITE TOY: TENNIS BALL
OBSESSION: THE GOLF CART
NAUGHTIEST DEED: TRYING
TO BITE THE GOLF CART TIRES
WHILE THE GOLF CART IS MOVING
OWNER: NANCY PARKER WILSON
PET PEEVE: NOT GETTING THE FRONT SEAT

LABRADOODLE 4, BULLMASTIFF 3, & ENGLISH SPRINGER SPANIEL 2 | GREENVALE VINEYARDS, PORTSMOUTH, RI 255

SAMPSON

OBSESSION: EAR RUBS
KNOWN ACCOMPLICE: DELILAH
PET PEEVE: HAVING HIS EARS CLEANED
FAVORITE TOY: STUFFED SQUEAKY DUCK
OWNERS: PATRICK AND KRISTEN DUFFELER
FAVORITE PASTIME: WALKING DOWN TO THE RIVER

DELILAH

OBSESSION: BELLY RUBS
PET PEEVE: THE ELECTRIC FENCE
FAVORITE TOYS: OTHER DOGS OR PUPPIES
OWNERS: PATRICK AND KRISTEN DUFFELER
NAUGHTIEST DEED: STEALING A PIECE OF
LONDON BROIL FROM THE KITCHEN COUNTER
FAVORITE PASTIME: WALKING DOWN TO THE RIVER

THE WILLIAMSBURG WINERY WILLIAMSBURG, VA | GERMAN SHEPHERDS X, 2

ROXANNE

OWNER: BEN MOFFETT
FAVORITE TOY: PEOPLE
NAUGHTIEST DEED: TEARING UP TISSUES
AND NAPKINS SHE FINDS ON THE FLOOR
FAVORITE PASTIME: SITTING IN SOMEONE'S LAP
OBSESSION: BARKING AT THE IMAGINARY OWL
FAVORITE FOOD: ANYTHING INCLUDING BROCCOLI
PET PEEVE: NOT BEING PICKED UP AND CUDDLED

OWNER: BEN MOFFETT
PET PEEVE: HAVING TO STAY ALONE
NAUGHTIEST DEED: CHEWING ON HOUSE SHOES
FAVORITE TOY: HOUSE SHOES (GOOD FOR SITTING IN)
OBSESSION: DANCING FOR HIS MORNING BONE TREAT
FAVORITE FOOD: CHEESE – THE SMELLIER, THE BETTER
FAVORITE PASTIME: GOING ANYWHERE WITH HIS PEOPLE

STERLING

CHANCE

FAVORITE FOOD: FRENCH FRIES
FAVORITE TOY: BIG SOFT PULL TOY
FAVORITE PASTIME: DIGGING FOR SAGE RATS
OWNERS: WADE WOLFE AND BECKY YEAMAN
NAUGHTIEST DEED: RUNNING OFF WHEN HE GETS
LET OUTSIDE INSTEAD OF DOING HIS BUSINESS
OBSESSION: THE FEDEX GUY BECAUSE HE BRINGS TREATS

THURSTON WOLFE WINERY PROSSER, WA | AIREDALE TERRIER, 4

HN DEERE

OWNER: DAN RINKE
OBSESSION: HERDING
FAVORITE PASTIME: HERDING FORKLIFTS
PET PEEVE: DIZZY NOT PLAYING WITH HER
NAUGHTIEST DEEDS: CHASING CATS AND TAUNTING DIZZY

OWNER: DAN RINKE
PET PEEVE: BEING LEFT ALONE
FAVORITE FOOD: RAWHIDE BONES
NAUGHTIEST DEED: DIGGING HOLES
FAVORITE PASTIME: CHASING GOPHERS
OBSESSIONS: GOPHERS AND PLAYING BALL

DIZZY

AUSTRALIAN SHEPHERD, 3 & SPRINGER SPANIEL, 8 | **JOHAN VINEYARDS** RICKREALL, OR | 259

DUNCAN

OWNER: JOHN FREEMAN
FAVORITE TOY: TUG-A-WAR ROPE
KNOWN ACCOMPLICES: SUGAR AND DUDE
OBSESSION: RETRIEVING WHATEVER YOU THROW
FAVORITE PASTIME: BEING A PROFESSIONAL PHEASANT CHASER
PET PEEVES: SMALL DOGS, SMALL CHILDREN AND SMALL PORTIONS
NAUGHTIEST DEED: NABBING A FULLY COOKED CORNED BEEF OFF THE KITCHEN COUNTER

OBSESSION: LARGE BIRDS
OWNER: FRANK ALTAMURA
FAVORITE PASTIMES: RUNNING AFTER
SHEEP AND CHASING WILD TURKEYS
PET PEEVES: CLOSE-UPS AND STRANGERS
NAUGHTIEST DEED: JUMPING OVER FENCES
KNOWN ACCOMPLICES: FRANK AND GIANCARLO
FAVORITE TOYS: SOCK MONKEY AND BIG BONES

JARNO

CHANCE

FAVORITE FOOD: PISTACHIOS
OWNERS: DAVID AND CINDY LAWSON
FAVORITE PASTIME: MEETING GUESTS
WHO COME TO SEE HIM AT THE WINERY
PET PEEVES: THE WORDS "LEAVE IT" AND "NO"
NAUGHTIEST DEED: STEALING BUNGS OUT OF FULL
BARRELS OF WINE WHEN HE DOESN'T HAVE A BALL

PET PEEVE: DIETS
OBSESSION: FOOD
FAVORITE PASTIME: BEING
PETTED BY GUESTS AT THE WINERY
NAUGHTIEST DEED: STEALING FOOD
OWNERS: DAVID AND CINDY LAWSON

STARR

COVINGTON CELLARS WOODINVILLE, WA | HUNGARIAN VIZSLAS, 5 & 10

KNOWN ACCOMPLICE: WILLOW
OBSESSION: LYING SPREAD-
EAGLED IN FRONT OF CUSTOMERS
FAVORITE TOY: BIG GREEN FROG
OWNERS: CHARLIE AND PEGGY BECKER
FAVORITE PASTIME: GOING TO LOWES
AND RIDING ON THE BLUE PUSH CART
NAUGHTIEST DEED: CHEWING THE SHRUBS

MÜLLER

ROSEBUD

PET PEEVE: CYCLISTS
OWNER: JEAN-FRANÇOIS PELLET
OBSESSION: CHASING GOPHERS
FAVORITE TOY: ANYTHING THAT SHE CAN CHEW
KNOWN ACCOMPLICES: THE NEIGHBOR'S DOGS
NAUGHTIEST DEED: CHASING AND GETTING SPRAYED BY SKUNKS

PEPPER BRIDGE WINERY WALLA WALLA, WA | BORDER COLLIE X, 2

FAVORITE FOOD: MEATBALLS
OWNER: MATTHEW BEVERLY
FAVORITE TOY: HIS OLD TUG-O-WAR ROPE
KNOWN ACCOMPLICE: THE LITTLE LEBOWSKI, THE BLACK KITTEN
OBSESSIONS: HIS THREE KITTENS AND SHADY SPOTS ON A SUMMER DAY
NAUGHTIEST DEED: CARRYING THE CATS AROUND BY THE SCRUFF OF THEIR NECK
PET PEEVES: HANDSHAKES THAT LAST A BIT TOO LONG AND TALL MEN WITH HATS

ROMEO

GERMAN SHEPHERD X, 3 | **HOPE & GRACE WINES** YOUNTVILLE, CA

CRISTO

OWNER: MARK NESBITT

FAVORITE PASTIME:
CHASING BARREL BUNGS

OBSESSIONS: SQUIRRELS
AND BARREL BUNGS

FAVORITE TOY: BARREL BUNG

NAUGHTIEST DEED: EATING
THE BREAKFAST BACON

FERGIE

PET PEEVE: SQUIRRELS

OWNER: HARRIGAN NESBITT

FAVORITE PASTIME:
DESTROYING SOCCER BALLS

NAUGHTIEST DEED:
SLEEPING ON THE COUCH

FAVORITE FOOD: WATERMELON

BLUE

PET PEEVE: BIRDS

OBSESSION: PEOPLE
AT THE FRONT DOOR

NAUGHTIEST DEED:
SLEEPING ON THE COUCH

OWNER: MACKENNA NESBITT

FAVORITE FOOD: PEANUT BUTTER

CHUMEIA VINEYARDS PASO ROBLES, CA | GOLDEN RETRIEVER, 6, AUSTRALIAN SHEPHERD X, 3 & BORDER COLLIE X, 5

OWNERS: THE PILGRIM FAMILY
KNOWN ACCOMPLICE: THOMAS THE WINERY CAT
OBSESSIONS: RABBITS AND GROUND SQUIRRELS
FAVORITE FOODS: PORK CHOPS AND PEANUT BUTTER
FAVORITE TOY: A MOSTLY EMPTY PEANUT BUTTER JAR
NAUGHTIEST DEED: STEALING NEW STAFF MEMBERS' FOOD
FAVORITE PASTIMES: EATING AND HANGING OUT WITH HIS FAMILY

KASEY

ITALY'S HIDDEN TREASURES... IN KALAMAZOO

Christine Skandis is so passionate about the promotion and protection of Italian heirloom wines that she has named most of her seven beloved Bichon Frise after them. The wines are indigenous grape varietals that have been on the verge of extinction, and like Christine's pooches, are rare, unique and full of individual character. Okay everyone, smile for the camera ... everyone say formaggio!

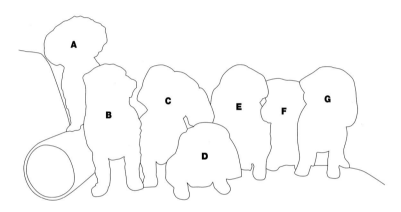

A PRINCESS BIANCA AGE: 9
FAVORITE PASTIME: HUGGING
OBSESSION: HUGGING YOU BY RUBBING
HER NECK AGAINST YOUR NECK
FAVORITE TOY: THE SPRINKLER
FAVORITE FOOD: ORGANIC BABY CARROTS

B PRINCE BAROLO AGE: 9
OBSESSION: KEEPING HIS EYE ON
HIS BROTHER, PRINCE DOLCETTO
FAVORITE TOY: SOCKS, SOCKS, SOCKS
FAVORITE PASTIME: NURSING ON CHRISTINE'S ARM

C PRINCESS ERBALUCE AGE: 7
FAVORITE TOY: BOODA STUFFED ELEPHANT
OBSESSION: SITTING UP ON HER HIND LEGS AND
BEGGING WITH HER FRONT PAWS LIKE A RABBIT
FAVORITE FOOD: MORSELS OF FOOD
LEFT ON PLATES IN THE DISHWASHER

D JE T'AIME AGE: 9
FAVORITE TOY: THE CAPTAIN'S
CHAIR OVERLOOKING THE WATER
OBSESSION: STICKING HER TONGUE OUT
FAVORITE PASTIMES: SUNBATHING AND SLEEPING

E PRINCESS PASSITO AGE: 7
OBSESSION: BEING SWEET (SHE
IS NAMED AFTER A DESSERT WINE)
FAVORITE TOY: THE SPRINKLER
FAVORITE FOOD: FLAXSEED VITAMINS
FAVORITE PASTIME: CHASING
BIRDS, SQUIRRELS AND HER TAIL

F PRINCESS BOMBINO AGE: 7
FAVORITE TOY: ANY TOY THAT
SHE CAN CARRY AND HIDE
FAVORITE FOOD: FROZEN ORGANIC KALE
FAVORITE PASTIME: WALKING ON THE BEACH
OBSESSION: CRYING EVERY DAY AT 5PM SO
SHE CAN GO FOR A WALK ON THE BEACH

G PRINCE DOLCETTO AGE: 9
OBSESSION: KEEPING HIS EYE ON
HIS BROTHER, PRINCE BAROLO
FAVORITE TOY: HIS STUFFED SNAKE
FAVORITE PASTIME: HANGING HIS
HEAD OVER THE DECK WAITING FOR
ANOTHER DOG TO GO BY

BANDIT

OWNER: SHIRLEY ARCHER
PET PEEVE: PACKED SUITCASES
FAVORITE TOY: SQUEAKY REINDEER
OBSESSIONS: SHIRLEY AND HIS SQUEAKY TOYS
KNOWN ACCOMPLICES: DENALI, BEAR AND WANAGI
FAVORITE FOODS: LIMA BEANS, SWEET POTATO AND CORN BREAD
NAUGHTIEST DEED: STEALING TOYS FROM THE THREE-YEAR-OLD GRANDSON

BRIGHT MEADOWS FARM NATHALIE, VA | PEKINGESE, 10

OWNER: JARED GERMAIN
FAVORITE FOOD: SAUSAGE PATTIES
PET PEEVE: LOUD, EXPLOSIVE NOISES
FAVORITE PASTIME: GRABBING ALL THE
ATTENTION HE CAN GET FROM VISITORS
OBSESSION: ACQUIRING AS MANY PETTING
HANDS ON HIS HEAD AS EARTHLY POSSIBLE
NAUGHTIEST DEED: CONSTANT PAWING AT JARED
FOR ATTENTION WHILE THEY DRIVE TO WORK

MAX

PET PEEVE: AN EMPTY FOOD BOWL
OWNERS: NICKI AND GEORGE BAZACO
FAVORITE PASTIMES: FOLLOWING NICKI
AROUND AND GREETING CUSTOMERS
KNOWN ACCOMPLICE: MUCH-MISSED LUCY
FAVORITE FOOD: ANYTHING AND EVERYTHING
OBSESSION: ALWAYS HAVING TO TAKE ONE OF HIS TOYS OUTSIDE

FAVORITE TOY: THE SQUEAKY RHINO
OBSESSION: TAUNTING RAVEN THE CAT
PET PEEVE: WHEN CORKY TAKES HIS TOYS
KNOWN ACCOMPLICE: CORKY, THE SENIOR
VINEYARD DOG AND CO-CONSPIRATOR
OWNERS: EMILY WILLIAMS AND CHARLIE DANERI
NAUGHTIEST DEED: REMOVING THE POPSICLE STICKS
THAT IDENTIFIED WHAT WAS GROWING IN THE GARDEN
FAVORITE PASTIME: PLAYING WITH ANYONE WHO WILL PLAY WITH HIM

COOPER

FAVORITE FOOD: TIDBITS
OWNER: JASON DAMIANOS
FAVORITE TOYS: SQUEAKY
ELEPHANT AND JASON'S SOCKS
PET PEEVE: THE BABYDOLL SHEEP
GETTING MORE ATTENTION THAN HER
NAUGHTIEST DEED: BITING OFF BUTTONS
FAVORITE PASTIME: PESTERING SPARTACUS

FAVORITE FOOD: TIDBITS
OWNER: JASON DAMIANOS
OBSESSION: RUNNING AFTER CLEOPATRA
PET PEEVE: COLD LONG ISLAND MORNINGS
KNOWN ACCOMPLICES: JASON AND CLEOPATRA
FAVORITE TOYS: SOCKS AND SQUEAKY ANIMALS
FAVORITE PASTIME: WRESTLING WITH CLEOPATRA

JASON'S VINEYARD JAMESPORT, NY | MALTESE TERRIERS, 9 MONTHS & 10 MONTHS

STATS, FACTS & WOOFILEAKS...

by Craig McGill

WE OFTEN GET ASKED QUESTIONS about the production of our books. Some are easy to answer and some require a more diplomatic response. "Is Nigel the smartest dog you've ever met?" or "Will Beatrice be on the cover?" usually tests our ability to keep a straight face but it's hard when our job is so much fun... after all, aren't they all cover worthy? We never 'out' any of the more difficult hounds or owners and all names have been changed to protect the innocent. Here are some of the 'facts' relating to the production of Wine Dogs USA 3:

- *Number of days of photography: 88*

- *Miles traveled by car: 14,208*

- *Miles traveled by plane: 238,857*

- *Number of States visited: 23 (Alaska, Arizona, Arkansas, California seven times, Connecticut, Delaware, Illinois, Indiana, Maryland, Massachusetts, Michigan, Nevada, New Jersey, New Mexico, New York, Oregon twice, Pennsylvania, Rhode Island, Tennessee, Texas, Utah, Virginia and Washington)*

- *Amount of Alaskan Wine Dogs: nil*

- *Amount of times we got lost: nil*

- *Amount of wrong turns: &*%$#*!!!*

- *Amount of destroyed clothing: 3 shirts, 1 leather jacket, 2 shoelaces*

- *Most common dog breed: Labrador (57)*

- *Least common breed: Flying technicolor circus hound (nil)*

- *Number of wineries featured in this edition: 190*

- *Total number of dogs photographed for this edition: 313*

- *Number of wineries visited worldwide by Wine Dogs: 1,884 (as of June 2012)*

- *Number of dogs referred to by the owner as 'gifted' or a 'genius': 33*

- *Number of dogs that couldn't sit when asked: 156*

- *Number of pedigree dogs: 47*

- *Number of rescue dogs: 146*

- *Number of dogs with their own Twitter account: 12*

- *Number of dogs with their own Facebook account: 19*

- *Number of dogs with their own winery: 1*

- *Number of goats photographed: 1*

- *Number of winemakers who dressed in a dog costume: 1*

- *Number of times the photographer didn't notice the dog was a winemaker dressed in a dog costume: 1*

- *Number of dogs with botox or cosmetic surgery: 4*

- *Number of times the photographer was bitten by a dog: nil*

- *Number of times the photographer was bitten by the owner: 2*

- *Number of times the photographer bit the dog: 1*

- *Most common dog names: Bella (6) and Riley (6)*

- *Number of dogs named after grape varieties: 6*

- *Number of dogs named after philosphers: 1*

- *Number of bottles of wine gifted by generous wineries: 312*

- *Number of wines tasted: 1,160*

- *Number of dogs with lingerie fetishes: 4*

- *Number of dogs that drink wine or eat grapes (not recommended for health reasons): 43*

- *Favorite restaurant: Red Ginger, Traverse City MI*

- *Favorite brewpub: Golden Valley, McMinnville OR*

- *Favorite bakery: Bouchon Bakery, Yountville CA*

- *Favorite pizza: Grana, Jamesport, Long Island NY*

- *Favorite wine bar: Vintner's Collective, Napa CA*

- *Favorite lunch restaurant: Cindy's Backstreet Kitchen, St. Helena CA*

- *Favorite café: Nick's Italian Café, McMinnville OR*

- *Favorite coffee shop: Walla Walla Roastery, Walla Walla WA*

- *Favorite record store: Waterloo, Austin TX*

- *Most original dog name: Leroy Garfunkel, Vina Robles, Paso Robles CA*

- *Number of dogs that have their own business cards: 3*

- *Number of dogs that have eaten furniture or electrical appliances: 5*

- *Number of dogs with only three legs: 1*

- *Number of dogs 'turned-on' by being photographed: 15*

PHOTOGRAPHY

Craig with Bones from Keever Vineyards, Yountville CA

PHOTOGRAPHY © CRAIG McGILL 2012

SUSAN ELLIOTT

SYDNEY, NSW

Stella and Sue

SUSAN IS A MULTI-SKILLED ARTIST WITH A BACKGROUND IN FINE ART, ILLUSTRATION AND PRINTMAKING. AFTER COMPLETING TWO YEARS OF A PSYCHOLOGY DEGREE, SUE CHANGED TO A CAREER IN ART. SHE GRADUATED FROM THE CITY ART INSTITUTE IN 1986, MAJORING IN DRAWING, PRINTMAKING AND PAINTING.

AFTER TWO YEARS LIVING ABROAD, SUE RETURNED TO AUSTRALIA AND EXHIBITED HER GRAPHIC ART AND SCREENPRINTS EXTENSIVELY AROUND SYDNEY, WHILE ALSO WORKING IN A NUMBER OF SMALL DESIGN STUDIOS. SHE HAS DEVELOPED INTO AN AWARD-WINNING GRAPHIC DESIGNER WITH OVER 20 YEARS OF EXPERIENCE IN THE INDUSTRY.

SUE JOINED McGILL DESIGN GROUP IN 1999 AS CO-OWNER AND CREATIVE DIRECTOR. SHE IS ALSO CO-FOUNDER AND PRINCIPAL OF THE GIANT DOG PUBLISHING HOUSE, WHICH IS RESPONSIBLE FOR PRODUCING A NUMBER OF BEST-SELLING BOOKS, INCLUDING THE WINE DOGS TITLES.

FAVORITE FOOD: NOODLES
FAVORITE PASTIME: WATCHING '70s AUSTRALIAN FILMS
KNOWN ACCOMPLICES: THE CLOWN LOACHES
OBSESSIONS: BATH SALTS AND CRYPTIC CROSSWORDS
PET HATES: WHISTLING AND RAISIN TOAST WITH PEEL

SUE'S KNOWLEDGE OF DOGS IS UNPARALLELED, AND IN THE PAST SHE HAS ALSO FOUND TIME TO BE A SUCCESSFUL SIBERIAN HUSKY BREEDER. ALTHOUGH CURRENTLY DOGLESS, SUE LOVES TO SPEND TIME WITH THE MANY WINE DOGS SHE MEETS FROM AROUND THE WORLD. SUE IS A LOVER OF WINE AND USUALLY REACHES FOR HER FAVORITE RIESLING OR PINOT NOIR WHEN FEELING A LITTLE HUSKY.

GIANT DOG PUBLISHING

GIANT DOG IS A NICHE INDEPENDENT PUBLISHING HOUSE SPECIALISING IN PRODUCING BENCHMARK QUALITY DESIGN AND ART BOOKS. RECENT PUBLICATIONS INCLUDE *WINE DOGS USA* 3, *WINE DOGS AUSTRALIA* 3, *WINE DOGS ITALY*, *WINE DOGS NEW ZEALAND* AND *FOOTY DOGS*.
www.giantdog.com.au

CRAIG McGILL

SYDNEY, NSW

ORIGINALLY FROM SHEPPARTON, VICTORIA, CRAIG IS A SELF-TAUGHT DESIGNER AND ILLUSTRATOR WHO STARTED HIS OWN DESIGN BUSINESS IN MELBOURNE AT 18 YEARS OF AGE. DURING THAT TIME HE WAS APPOINTED AS A DESIGN CONSULTANT TO THE RESERVE BANK OF AUSTRALIA.

HIS DESIGNS AND ILLUSTRATIONS HAVE GRACED BANKNOTES THROUGHOUT THE WORLD, INCLUDING THE AUSTRALIAN BICENTENARY TEN-DOLLAR NOTE. HIS WORK APPEARS ON THE ORIGINAL AUSTRALIAN $100 NOTE, PAPUA NEW GUINEA KINA, COOK ISLAND DOLLARS AND ENGLISH POUND TRAVELLER'S CHEQUES. CRAIG WAS ALSO INVOLVED IN THE DESIGN AND ILLUSTRATION OF MANY COUNTRIES' SECURITY DOCUMENTS SUCH AS PASSPORTS, BONDS AND TRAVELLER'S CHEQUES.

AT THE AGE OF 23 HE DESIGNED THE ENTIRE SERIES OF THE COOK ISLAND BANKNOTES AND IT IS BELIEVED THAT HE WAS THE WORLD'S YOUNGEST DESIGNER TO DESIGN A COUNTRY'S COMPLETE CURRENCY. IN 1991, CRAIG MOVED TO SYDNEY WHERE HIS ILLUSTRATIONS WERE REGULARLY COMMISSIONED BY AGENCIES AND DESIGNERS BOTH IN AUSTRALIA AND AROUND THE WORLD.

Craig and Tarka

DATE OF BIRTH: DEAD IN DOG YEARS

FAVORITE FOOD: ROAST DUCK AND PINOT NOIR

FAVORITE PASTIMES: VENTRILOQUISM AND BEING A BIG KID

NAUGHTIEST DEED: CHASING HUSKIES WHILE STARK NAKED

OBSESSIONS: BEER, WINE AND COLLECTING USELESS THINGS

KNOWN ACCOMPLICES: THE VOICES IN MY HEAD

PET HATE: UNORIGINAL IDEAS

HE IS NOW WIDELY KNOWN AS AUSTRALIA'S ONLY FREELANCE CURRENCY DESIGNER. CRAIG HAS ALSO DESIGNED AND ILLUSTRATED NINE STAMPS FOR AUSTRALIA POST.

CRAIG HAS BEEN CREATIVE DIRECTOR OF HIS OWN AGENCY, McGILL DESIGN GROUP, FOR OVER TWENTY-FIVE YEARS.

HAVING GROWN UP WITH A SUCCESSION OF BEAGLES AND HUSKIES, CRAIG IS CURRENTLY ROAD-TESTING SEVERAL HUNDRED DOG BREEDS FROM WINERIES AROUND THE WORLD. www.realnasty.com.au

McGILL DESIGN GROUP

McGILL DESIGN GROUP WAS FORMED IN 1981 AND SPECIALISES IN PROVIDING A WIDE RANGE OF QUALITY GRAPHIC DESIGN SERVICES. THE STUDIO HAS PRODUCED NUMEROUS FINE WINE LABELS AND PACKAGING AS WELL AS CORPORATE IDENTITIES, ADVERTISING, PUBLICATIONS AND TELEVISION COMMERCIALS. www.mcgilldesigngroup.com

WINERY AND VINEYARD LISTINGS

ARIZONA

1. ***Alcantara Vineyard
and Winery*** PAGES 122, 123
*7500 E. Alcantara Way,
Cottonwood AZ 86326
Ph: 928 649 8463
www.alcantaravineyard.com*

2. ***Javèlina Leap Vineyard
and Winery*** PAGES 152, 153
*1565 N. Page Springs Rd,
Cornville AZ 86325
Ph: 928 649 2681
www.javelinaleapwinery.com*

3. ***Kief-Joshua Vineyards*** PAGE 77
*370 Elgin Rd, Elgin AZ 85611
Ph: 520 455 5582
www.kj-vineyards.com*

4. ***Oak Creek Vineyards
and Winery*** PAGE 201
*1555 N. Page Springs Rd,
Cornville AZ 86325
Ph: 928 649 0290
www.oakcreekvineyards.net*

5. ***Rancho Rossa Vineyards***
PAGES 204, 205
*32 Cattle Ranch Lane, Elgin AZ 85611
Ph: 520 455 0700
www.ranchorossa.com*

6. ***Sonoita Vineyards*** PAGES 226, 227
*290 Elgin-Canelo Rd, Elgin AZ 85611
Ph: 520 455 5893
www.sonoitavineyards.com*

CALIFORNIA

1. *Alexander Valley Vineyards*
PAGE 250
8644 Hwy 128,
Healdsburg CA 95448
Ph: 707 433 7209
www.avvwine.com

2. *Alta Maria Vineyards*
PAGE 103
2933 Grand Ave, Suite A
Los Olivos CA 93441
Ph: 805 686 1144
www.altamaria.com

3. *Altamura Vineyards
and Winery* PAGE 261
1700 Wooden Valley Rd,
Napa CA 94558
Ph: 707 253 2000
www.altamura.com

4. *Amista Vineyards*
PAGE 199
3320 Dry Creek Rd,
Healdsburg CA 95448
Ph: 707 431 9200
www.amistavineyards.com

5. *Amizetta Winery*
PAGES 248, 249
1099 Greenfield Rd,
St. Helena CA 94574
Ph: 707 963 1460
www.amizetta.com

6. *Andrew Lane Winery* PAGES 188, 189
742 Sunnyside Rd,
St. Helena CA 94574
Ph: 707 815 3501
www.andrewlanewines.com

7. *Au Sommet Winery* PAGES 55–57
4400 Atlas Peak Rd,
Napa CA 94558
Ph: 707 251 9300
www.ausommetwine.com

8. *B. R. Cohn Winery* PAGES 24–26
15000 Sonoma Hwy,
Glen Ellen CA 95442
Ph: 707 938 4064
www.brcohn.com

9. *Bella Luna Winery* PAGE 114
1850 Templeton Rd,
Templeton CA 93465
Ph: 805 434 5477
www.bellalunawinery

10. *Benziger Family Winery*
PAGES 172–174
1883 London Ranch Rd,
Glen Ellen CA 95442
Ph: 888 490 2739
www.benziger.com

11. *Bianchi Winery* PAGE 116
3380 Branch Rd, Paso Robles CA 93466
Ph: 805 226 9922
www.bianchiwine.com

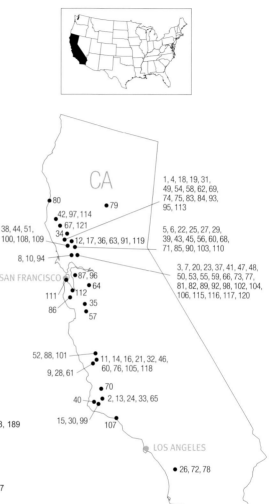

CA

1, 4, 18, 19, 31,
49, 54, 58, 62, 69,
74, 75, 83, 84, 93,
95, 113

80

79

42, 97, 114

38, 44, 51,
100, 108, 109

67, 121

34

12, 17, 36, 63, 91, 119

5, 6, 22, 25, 27, 29,
39, 43, 45, 56, 60, 68,
71, 85, 90, 103, 110

8, 10, 94

SAN FRANCISCO

87, 96

64

3, 7, 20, 23, 37, 41, 47, 48,
50, 53, 55, 59, 66, 73, 77,
81, 82, 89, 92, 98, 102, 104,
106, 115, 116, 117, 120

111

112

86

35

57

52, 88, 101

11, 14, 16, 21, 32, 46,
60, 76, 105, 118

9, 28, 61

70

40

2, 13, 24, 33, 65

15, 30, 99

107

LOS ANGELES

26, 72, 78

12. Brian Arden Wines PAGE 190
PO Box 96, Calistoga CA 94515
Ph: 707 637 3655
www.brianardenwines.com

13. Bridlewood Estate Winery PAGE 59
3555 Roblar Ave, Santa Ynez CA 93460
Ph: 805 688 9000
www.bridlewoodwinery.com

14. Brochelle Vineyards PAGE 119
2323 Tuley Rd, Paso Robles CA 93446
Ph: 805 237 4410
www.brochelle.com

15. Buttonwood Farm Winery PAGES 48, 49
1500 Alamo Pintado Rd,
Solvang CA 93463
Ph: 805 688 3032
www.buttonwoodwinery.com

**16. Carmody McKnight
Estate Vineyards** PAGE 118
11240 Chimney Rock Rd,
Paso Robles CA 93446
Ph: 805 238 9392
www.carmodymcknight.com

17. Castello di Amorosa PAGE 146
4045 North St. Helena Hwy,
Calistoga CA 94515
Ph: 707 967 6272
www.castellodiamorosa.com

18. Chalk Hill Estate and Winery
PAGE 254
10300 Chalk Hill Rd,
Healdsburg CA 95448
Ph: 707 657 4839
www.chalkhill.com

19. Chateau Diana Winery PAGE 179
6195 Dry Creek Rd,
Healdsburg CA 95448
Ph: 707 433 6992
www.chateaud.com

20. Chimney Rock Winery PAGES 100, 101
5350 Silverado Trail, Napa CA 94558
Ph: 707 257 2641
www.chimneyrock.com

21. Chumeia Vineyards PAGE 266
8331 Hwy 46 East,
Paso Robles CA 93446
Ph: 805 226 0102
www.chumeiavineyards.com

22. Clif Family Winery PAGE 163
709 Main St, St. Helena CA 94574
Ph: 707 968 0625
www.cliffamilywinery.com

23. Clos Du Val PAGES 12, 13
5330 Silverado Trail, Napa CA 95404
Ph: 707 261 5200
www.closduval.com

24. Consilience & Tre Anelli Wines
PAGES 170, 171
2923 Grand Ave, Los Olivos CA 93441
Ph: 805 691 1020
www.consiliencewines.com

25. Cook Family Winery PAGE 213
264 Crystal Springs Rd,
St. Helena CA 94574
Ph: 707 963 7760
www.cookwinery.com

26. Cougar Vineyard and Winery PAGE 124
39870 De Portola Rd, Temecula CA 92592
Ph: 951 491 0825
www.cougarvineyards.com

27. Crocker & Starr Winery PAGE 125
700 Dowdell Lane, St. Helena CA 94574
Ph: 707 967 9111
www.crockerstarr.com

28. Cypher Winery PAGE 137
3750 Hwy 46 West, Templeton CA 93465
Ph: 805 237 0055
www.cypherwinery.com

29. Dana Estates PAGE 192
P.O. Box 153, Rutherford CA 94573
www.danaestates.com

30. Dascomb Cellars PAGES 28, 29
1659 Copenhagen Drive,
Solvang CA 93463
Ph: 805 691 9175
www.dascombcellars.com

31. Del Carlo Winery PAGE 151
4939 Dry Creek Rd,
Healdsburg CA 95448
Ph: 707 484 2430
www.delcarlowinery.com

32. Dover Canyon Winery PAGES 4, 120
4520 Vineyard Drive,
Paso Robles CA 93446
Ph: 805 237 0101
www.dovercanyon.com

33. Dragonette Cellars PAGE 102
2445 Alamo Pintado Ave,
Los Olivos CA 93441
Ph: 805 693 0077
www.dragonettecellars.com

34. Dutcher Crossing Winery PAGE 58
8533 Dry Creek Rd, Geyserville CA 95441
Ph: 707 431 2700
www.dutchercrossingwinery.com

35. Emilio Guglielmo Winery PAGE 35
1480 East Main Ave,
Morgan Hill CA 95037
Ph: 408 779 2145
www.guglielmowinery.com

36. Envy Wines PAGE 149
1170 Tubbs Lane, Calistoga CA 94515
Ph: 707 942 4670
www.envywines.com

37. Falcor Winery PAGE 121
2511 Napa Valley Corporate Drive,
Suite 115, Napa CA 94558
Ph: 707 255 6070
www.falcorwines.com

38. Fisher Vineyards PAGE 184
6200 St. Helena Rd, Santa Rosa CA 95404
Ph: 707 539 7511
www.fishervineyards.com

39. Fleury Estate Winery PAGE 113
950 Galleron Rd, Rutherford CA 94573
Ph: 707 967 8333
www.fleurywinery.com

40. Foley Family Wines PAGE 195
6121 E. Hwy 246, Lompoc CA 93436
Ph: 805 737 6222
www.foleywines.com

41. Fortunati Vineyards PAGE 112
986 Salvador Ave, Napa CA 94558
Ph: 707 255 9300
www.fortunativineyards.com

42. Foursight Wines PAGE 63
14475 Hwy 128, Boonville CA 95415
Ph: 707 895 2889
www.foursightwines.com

43. Frenchie Winery PAGES 244–246
849 Zinfandel Lane, St. Helena CA 94574
Ph: 707 963 6948
www.frenchiewinery.com

44. Graton Ridge Cellars PAGE 23
3561 Gravenstein Hwy N,
Sebastopol CA 95472
Ph: 707 823 3040
www.gratonridge.com

45. Heibel Ranch Vineyards PAGES 68, 223
1241 Adams St, # 1043,
St. Helena CA 94574
Ph: 707 968 9289
www.heibelranch.com

46. Herman Story Winery PAGES 108–110
1227 Paso Robles St,
Paso Robles CA 93446
Ph: 805 237 2400
www.hermanstorywines.com

47. Hess Collection, The PAGES 98, 99
4411 Redwood Rd, Napa CA 94558
Ph: 707 255 1144
www.hesscollection.com

48. Hill Family Estate PAGE 111
6512 Washington St,
Yountville CA 94599
Ph: 707 944 9580
www.hillfamilyestate.com

49. HKG Estate Wines PAGE 16
6050 Westside Rd, Healdsburg CA 95448
Ph: 707 433 6491
www.hkgwines.com

50. Hope & Grace Wines PAGE 265
6540 Washington St,
Yountville CA 94599
Ph: 707 944 2500
www.hopeandgracewines.com

**51. Inspiration Vineyards
and Winery** PAGE 200
3360 Coffey Lane,
Santa Rosa CA 95403
Ph: 707 237 4980
www.inspirationvineyards.com

52. J & J Cellars PAGE 208
2850 Ranchita Canyon Rd,
San Miguel CA 93451
Ph: 805 467 2891
www.jjcellars.com

53. Jessup Cellars PAGE 147
6740 Washington St,
Yountville CA 94599
Ph: 707 944 8523
www.jessupcellars.com

54. Jordan Winery PAGES 126, 127
1474 Alexander Valley Rd,
Healdsburg CA 95448
Ph: 800 654 1213
www.jordanwinery.com

55. **Keever Vineyards** PAGE 14
PO Box 2906, Yountville CA 94599
Ph: 707 944 0910
www.keevervineyards.com

56. **Kelham Vineyards** PAGES 50, 51
360 Zinfandel Lane, St. Helena CA 94574
Ph: 707 963 2000
www.kelhamvineyards.com

57. **Kirigin Cellars** PAGE 97
11550 Watsonville Rd, Gilroy CA 95020
Ph: 408 847 8827
www.kirigincellars.com

58. **Kokomo Winery** PAGES 52–54
4791 Dry Creek Rd, Healdsburg CA 95448
Ph: 707 433 0205
www.kokomowinery.com

59. **Krupp Brothers Winery** PAGE 46
3267 Soda Canyon Rd, Napa CA 94558
Ph: 707 226 2215
www.kruppbrothers.com

60. **Kukkula** PAGES 60, 61
9515 Chimney Rock Rd,
Paso Robles CA 93446
Ph: 805 227 0111
www.kukkulawine.com

61. **Lago Giuseppe Winery** PAGES 176, 177
8345 Green Valley Rd,
Templeton CA 93465
Ph: 805 237 7300
www.lagogiuseppe.com

62. **Lambert Bridge Winery** PAGES 128–130
4085 West Dry Creek Rd,
Healdsburg CA 95448
Ph: 800 975 0555
www.lambertbridge.com

63. **Lava Vine Winery** PAGE 175
965 Silverado Trail, Calistoga CA 94515
Ph: 707 942 9500
www.lavavine.com

64. **Longevity Wines** PAGE 85
2271 S. Vasco Ste. B, Livermore CA 94550
Ph: 925 443 9463
www.longevitywines.com

65. **Longoria Wines** PAGE 166
2935 Grand Ave, Los Olivos CA 93441
Ph: 805 688 0305
www.longoriawine.com

66. **Ma(i)sonry** PAGE 43
6711 Washington St, Yountville CA 94599
Ph: 707 944 0889
www.maisonry.com

67. **Maple Creek Winery** PAGE 178
20799 Hwy 128, Yorkville CA 95494
Ph: 707 895 3001
www.maplecreekwine.com

68. **Markham Vineyards** PAGES 158, 159
2812 St. Helena Hwy North,
St. Helena CA 94574
Ph: 707 963 5292
www.markhamvineyards.com

69. **Martorana Family Winery** PAGE 197
5956 West Dry Creek Rd,
Healdsburg CA 95448
Ph: 707 433 1909
www.martoranafamilywinery.com

70. **McKeon-Phillips Winery** PAGE 36
2115 S. Blosser Rd, Suite 114,
Santa Maria CA 93458
Ph: 805 928 3025
www.mckeonphillipswinery.com

71. **Merryvale Vineyards** PAGE 198
1000 Main St, St. Helena CA 95474
Ph: 707 963 2225
www.merryvale.com

72. **Monte De Oro Winery** PAGE 64
35820 Rancho California Rd,
Temecula CA 92591
Ph: 951 491 6551
www.montedeoro.com

73. **Monticello Vineyards** PAGE 76
4242 Big Ranch Rd, Napa CA 94558
Ph: 707 253 2802
www.corleyfamilynapavalley.com

74. **Moshin Vineyards** PAGE 160
10295 Westside Rd,
Healdsburg CA 95448
Ph: 707 433 5499
www.moshinvineyards.com

75. **Mutt Lynch Winery** PAGE 131
602 Limerick Lane, Healdsburg CA 95448
Ph: 707 942 6180
www.muttlynchwinery.com

76. **Niner Wine Estates** PAGES 155–157
2400 Hwy 46 West,
Paso Robles CA 93446
Ph: 805 239 2233
www.ninerwine.com

77. **O'Brien Estate** PAGE 45
1200 Orchard Ave, Napa CA 94558
Ph: 707 252 8463
www.obrienestate.com

78. **Oak Mountain Winery** PAGE 219
    36522 Via Verde, Temecula CA 92592
    Ph: 951 699 9102
    www.oakmountainwinery.com

79. **Odyssey Winery**
    and Vineyards PAGE 206
    6237 Cohasset Rd, Chico CA 95973
    Ph: 530 891 9463

80. **Pacific Star Winery** PAGE 37
    33000 N Hwy 1, Fort Bragg CA 95437
    Ph: 707 964 1155
    www.pacificstarwinery.com

81. **Page Wine Cellars | Revolver Wine Co.**
    PAGE 236
    6505 Washington St,
    Yountville CA 95499
    Ph: 707 944 2339
    www.pagewinecellars.com
    www.revolverwines.com

82. **Palmaz Vineyards** PAGE 181
    4029 Hagen Rd, Napa CA 94558
    Ph: 707 226 5587
    www.palmazvineyards.com

83. **Papapietro Perry** PAGE 47
    4791 Dry Creek Rd, Healdsburg CA 95448
    Ph: 707 433 0422
    www.papapietro-perry.com

84. **Peterson Winery** PAGES 138, 139
    4791 Dry Creek Rd, Building 7,
    Healdsburg CA 95448
    Ph: 707 431 7568
    www.petersonwinery.com

85. **Pope Valley Winery** PAGE 96
    6613 Pope Valley Rd,
    Pope Valley CA 94567
    Ph: 707 965 1246
    www.popevalleywinery.com

86. **Portola Vineyards** PAGE 162
    850 Los Trancos Rd,
    Portola Valley CA 94028
    Ph: 650 332 4959
    www.portolavineyards.com

87. **R&B Cellars** PAGE 92
    Tasting Room: Alameda Vintners Club
    2301 Central Ave, Alameda CA 94501
    Ph: 510 749 8477
    www.rbcellars.com

88. **Ranchita Canyon Vineyard**
    PAGES 132, 133
    3439 Ranchita Canyon Rd,
    San Miguel CA 93451
    Ph: 805 467 9448
    www.ranchitacanyonvineyard.com

89. **Regusci Winery** PAGES 65–67
    5584 Silverado Trail, Napa CA 94574
    Ph: 707 254 0403
    www.regusciwinery.com

90. **Revana Family Vineyard** PAGE 210
    2930 St. Helena Hwy North,
    St. Helena CA 94574
    Ph: 707 967 8814
    www.revanawine.com

91. **Reverie** PAGE 15
    1520 Diamond Mountain Rd,
    Calistoga CA 94515
    Ph: 707 942 6800
    www.reveriewine.com

92. **Robert Mondavi Winery** PAGE 211
    Highway 29, Oakville CA 94562
    Ph: 888 766 6328
    www.robertmondavi.com

93. **Robert Rue Vineyard and Winery**
    PAGE 222
    1406 Wood Rd, Fulton CA 95439
    Ph: 707 578 1601
    www.robertruevineyard.com

94. **Roche Winery** PAGE 218
    122 West Spain St, Sonoma CA 95476
    Ph: 707 935 7115
    www.rochewinery.com

95. **Rochioli Winery** PAGE 216
    6192 Westside Rd, Healdsburg CA 95448
    Ph: 707 433 2305
    www.rochioliwinery.com

96. **Rock Wall Wine Company** PAGE 93
    2301 Monarch St, Building 24,
    Suite 300, Alameda CA 94501
    Ph: 510 522 5700
    www.rockwallwines.com

97. **Roederer Estate** PAGE 90
    4501 Highway 128, Philo CA 95466
    Ph: 707 895 2288
    www.roedererestate.net

98. **Rubicon Estate** PAGE 247
    1991 St. Helena Hwy,
    Rutherford CA 94573
    Ph: 707 968 1100
    www.rubiconestate.com

99. **Sevtap Winery** PAGES 88, 89
    1576 Copenhagen Drive #1,
    Solvang CA 93463
    Ph: 805 693 9200
    www.sevtapwinery.com

100. Sheldon Wines PAGES 214, 215
1301 Cleveland Ave,
Santa Rosa CA 95401
Ph: 707 865 6755
www.sheldonwines.com

101. Silver Horse Winery PAGES 38, 42
2995 Pleasant Rd, San Miguel CA 93451
Ph: 805 467 9463
www.silverhorse.com

102. Silver Oak Cellars PAGES 32–34
915 Oakville Cross Rd, Oakville CA 94562
Ph: 707 942 7022
www.silveroak.com

103. Spring Mountain Vineyard
PAGES 228, 229
2805 Spring Mountain Rd,
St. Helena CA 94574
Ph: 707 967 4188
www.springmountainvineyard.com

**104. St. Supéry Estate Vineyards
and Winery** PAGE 81
8440 St. Helena Hwy,
Rutherford CA 94573
Ph: 707 963 4507
www.stsupery.com
www.facebook.com/GG.CCO

105. Stacked Stone Cellars PAGES 234, 235
1525 Peachy Canyon Rd,
Paso Robles CA 93446
Ph: 805 238 7872
www.stackedstone.com

106. Stagecoach Vineyard PAGE 238
3267 Soda Canyon Rd, Napa CA 94558
Ph: 707 259 1198
www.stagecoachvineyard.com

107. Summerland Winery PAGE 80
2330 Lillie Ave, Summerland CA 93067
Ph: 805 565 9463
www.summerlandwine.com

108. Sunce Winery PAGE 91
1839 Olivet Rd, Santa Rosa CA 95401
Ph: 707 526 9463
www.suncewinery.com

109. Taft Street Winery PAGE 165
2030 Barlow Lane, Sebastopol CA 95472
Ph: 707 823 2049
www.taftstreetwinery.com

110. Terra Valentine PAGE 164
3787 Spring Mountain Rd,
St. Helena CA 94574
Ph: 707 967 8340
www.terravalentine.com

111. The Winery SF PAGE 78
200 California Ave, Building 180 N,
San Francisco CA 94130
Ph: 415 735 8423
www.winery-sf.com

112. Thomas Fogarty Winery PAGES 19–21
19501 Skyline Boulevard,
Woodside CA 94062
Ph: 650 851 6777
www.thomasfogartywinery.com

113. Thomas George Estates PAGE 18
8075 Westside Rd, Healdsburg CA 95448
Ph: 707 431 8031
www.thomasgeorgeestates.com

114. Toulouse Vineyards PAGES 134, 135
8001 Hwy 128, Philo CA 95466
Ph: 707 895 2828
www.toulousevineyards.com

115. Trefethen Family Vineyards
PAGES 86, 87
1160 Oak Knoll Ave, Napa CA 94558
Ph: 866 895 7696
www.trefethen.com

116. Truchard Vineyards PAGE 240
3234 Old Sonoma Rd, Napa CA 94559
Ph: 707 253 7153
www.truchardvineyards.com

117. Tusk Estates PAGE 212
Ph: 707 944 8355
www.tuskestates.com

118. Vina Robles PAGE 243
3700 Mill Rd, Paso Robles CA 93446
Ph: 805 227 4812
www.vinarobles.com

119. Vincent Arroyo Winery PAGE 79
2361 Greenwood Ave,
Calistoga CA 94515
Ph: 707 942 6995
www.vincentarroyo.com

120. Vintner's Collective PAGES 22, 154
1245 Main St, Napa CA 94559
Ph: 707 255 7150
www.vcnv.com

121. Yorkville Cellars PAGE 136
25701 Hwy 128, Yorkville CA 95494
Ph: 707 894 9177
www.yorkvillecellars.com

ILLINOIS

1. ***Fox Valley Winery*** PAGE 196
    5600 Route 34, Oswego IL 60543
    Ph: 630 554 0404
    www.foxvalleywinery.com

MARYLAND

1. ***Frederick Cellars*** PAGE 273
    221 North East St,
    Frederick MD 21701
    Ph: 301 668 0311
    www.frederickcellars.com

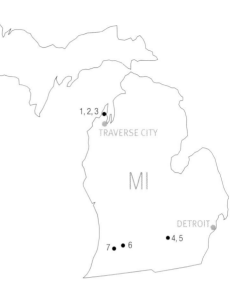

MICHIGAN

1. **Black Star Farms** PAGE 117
   10844 E. Revold Rd,
   Suttons Bay MI 49682
   Ph: 231 944 1250
   www.blackstarfarms.com

2. **Chateau Fontaine** PAGE 94
   2290 South French Rd,
   Lake Leelanau MI 49653
   Ph: 231 256 0000
   www.chateaufontaine.com

3. **Forty-Five North Vineyards
   and Winery** PAGES 186, 187
   8580 E. Horn Rd,
   Lake Leelanau MI 49653
   Ph: 231 271 1188
   www.fortyfivenorth.com

4. **Lone Oak Vineyard Estate** PAGE 11
   8400 Ann Arbor Rd,
   Grass Lake MI 49240
   Ph: 517 522 8167
   www.loneoakvineyards.com

5. **Sandhill Crane Vineyards** PAGE 217
   4724 Walz Rd, Jackson MI 49201
   Ph: 517 764 0679
   www.sandhillcranevineyards.com

6. **Skandis Fine Wines**
   PAGES 268, 269
   530 West South St,
   Kalamazoo MI 49007
   Ph: 269 998 9300
   www.SkandisFineWine.com
   www.RoyalWineCanines.com

7. **St. Julian Wine Co.** PAGE 231
   716 S. Kalamazoo St,
   Paw Paw MI 49079
   Ph: 269 657 5568
   www.stjulian.com

NEW YORK

1. **Castello di Borghese Winery**
PAGE 140
17150 County Route 48,
Cutchogue NY 11935
Ph: 631 734 5111
www.castellodiborghese.com

2. **Duck Walk Vineyards** PAGE 253
44535 Main Rd,
Southold NY 11971
Ph: 631 765 3500
www.duckwalk.com

3. **Jason's Vineyard** PAGE 274
1785 Main Rd, Jamesport NY 11947
Ph: 631 238 5801
www.jasonsvineyard.com

4. **Lenz Winery, The** PAGES 232, 233
38355 Main Rd, Peconic NY 11958
Ph: 631 734 6010
www.lenzwine.com

5. **Pindar Vineyards** PAGE 221
37645 Main Rd, Peconic NY 11958
Ph: 631 734 6200
www.pindar.net

6. **Red Hook Winery, The**
PAGES 75, 297
Pier 41, Suite 325A,
175–204 Van Dyke St,
Brooklyn NY 11231
Ph: 347 689 2432
www.redhookwinery.com

7. **Shinn Estate Vineyards** PAGE 145
2000 Oregon Rd,
Mattituck NY 11952
Ph: 631 804 0367
www.shinnestatevineyards.com

NY

1, 2, 4, 5, 7
3

NEW YORK

6

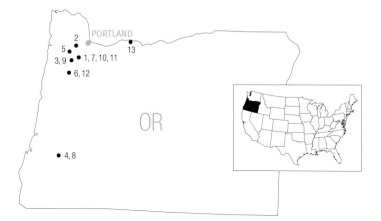

OREGON

1. **12th and Maple Wine Co.** PAGE 191
   1242 SE Maple St, Dundee OR 97115
   Ph: 503 538 7724

2. **A Blooming Hill Vineyard** PAGE 104
   5195 SW Hergert Rd,
   Cornelius OR 97113
   Ph: 503 992 1196
   www.abloominghillvineyard.com

3. **Anne Amie Vineyards** PAGE 161
   6580 NE Mineral Springs Rd,
   Carlton OR 97111
   Ph: 503 864 2991
   www.anneamie.com

4. **Becker Vineyard** PAGE 263
   360 Klahowya Lane,
   Roseburg OR 97471
   Ph: 541 677 0288
   www.beckerwine.com

5. **Big Table Farm** PAGE 115
   26851 NW Williams Canyon Rd,
   Gaston OR 97119
   Ph: 503 662 3129
   www.bigtablefarm.com

6. **Johan Vineyards** PAGE 259
   4285 N. Pacific Hwy, Rickreall OR 97371
   Ph: 866 379 6029
   www.johanvineyards.com

7. **Lange Estate** PAGES 105–107
   18380 Northeast Buena Vista Drive,
   Dundee OR 97115
   Ph: 503 538 6476
   www.langewinery.com

8. **Melrose Vineyards** PAGE 62
   885 Melqua Rd,
   Roseburg OR 97471
   Ph: 541 672 6080
   www.melrosevineyards.com

9. **Soter Vineyards** PAGE 225
   10880 NE Mineral Springs Rd,
   Carlton OR 97111
   Ph: 503 662 5600
   www.sotervineyards.com

10. **Styring Vineyards** PAGE 241
    19960 NE Ribbon Ridge Rd,
    Newberg OR 97132
    Ph: 503 866 6741
    www.styringvineyards.com

11. **Torii Mor** PAGE 17
    18365 NE Fairview Drive,
    Dundee OR 97115
    Ph: 503 554 0105
    www.toriimorwinery.com

12. **Van Duzer Vineyards** PAGE 44
    11975 Smithfield Rd,
    Dallas OR 97338
    Ph: 503 623 6420
    www.vanduzer.com

13. **Wy'East Vineyards** PAGE 242
    3189 Hwy 35, Hood River OR 97031
    Ph: 541 386 1277
    www.wyeastvineyards.com

RHODE ISLAND

1. ***Greenvale Vineyards*** PAGE 255
582 Wapping Rd,
Portsmouth RI 02871
Ph: 401 847 3777
www.greenvale.com

TEXAS

1. ***Lost Oak Winery***
PAGE 148
2116 FM 731
Burleson TX 76028
Ph: 817 426 6625
www.lostoakwinery.com

2. ***Stone House Vineyard*** PAGES 143, 144
24350 Haynie Flat Rd,
Spicewood TX 78669
Ph: 512 264 3630
www.stonehousevineyard.com

3. ***Zin Valle Vineyards*** PAGE 251
7315 Canutillo La Union Rd,
Canutillo TX 79835
Ph: 915 877 4544
www.zinvalle.com

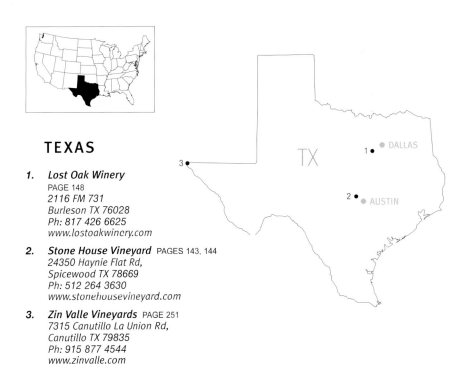

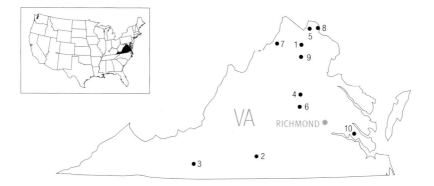

VIRGINIA

1. ***Barrel Oak Winery*** PAGES 182, 183
3623 Grove Lane, Delaplane VA 20144
Ph: 540 364 6402
www.barreloak.com

2. ***Bright Meadows Farm*** PAGE 270
1181 Nathalie Rd, Nathalie VA 24577
Ph: 434 349 5349
www.brightmeadowsfarm.com

3. ***Chateau Morrisette*** PAGE 141
287 Winery Rd SW, Floyd VA 24091
Ph: 540 593 2865
www.thedogs.com

4. ***Cooper Vineyards*** PAGES 30, 31
13372 Shannon Hill Rd,
Louisa VA 23093
Ph: 540 894 5474
www.coopervineyards.com

5. ***Doukenie Winery*** PAGE 272
14727 Mountain Rd, Hillsboro VA 20132
Ph: 540 668 6464
www.doukeniewinery.com

6. ***Grayhaven Winery*** PAGE 202
4675 E Grey Fox Circle,
Gum Spring VA 23065
Ph: 804 556 3917
www.grayhavenwinery.com

7. ***North Mountain Vineyard*** PAGE 220
4374 Swartz Rd, Maurertown VA 22644
Ph: 540 436 9463
www.northmountainvineyard.com

8. ***Tarara Winery*** PAGE 239
13648 Tarara Lane, Leesburg VA 20176
Ph: 703 771 7100
www.tarara.com

9. ***Unicorn Winery*** PAGE 83
489 Old Bridge Rd, Amissville VA 20106
Ph: 540 349 5885
www.unicornwinery.com

10. ***Williamsburg Winery, The*** PAGE 256
5800 Wessex Hundred,
Williamsburg VA 23185
Ph: 757 229 0999
www.williamsburgwinery.com

WASHINGTON

1. **Airfield Estates** PAGE 185
560 Merlot Drive, Prosser WA 99350
Ph: 509 786 7401
www.airfieldwines.com

2. **Amavi Cellars** PAGE 84
3796 Peppers Bridge Rd,
Walla Walla WA 99362
Ph: 509 525 3541
www.amavicellars.com

3. **Bergevin Lane Vineyards** PAGE 180
1215 West Poplar St,
Walla Walla WA 99362
Ph: 509 526 4300
www.bergevinlane.com

4. **Cascade Cliffs Vineyard
& Winery** PAGE 271
8866 Hwy 14, Wishram WA 98673
Ph: 509 767 1100
www.cascadecliffs.com

5. **Covington Cellars** PAGE 262
18580 142nd Ave NE,
Woodinville WA 98072
Ph: 425 806 8636
www.covingtoncellars.com

6. **Desert Wind Winery** PAGE 237
2258 Wine Country Rd,
Prosser WA 99350
Ph: 509 786 7277
www.desertwindwinery.com

7. **Dunham Cellars** PAGE 230
150 East Boeing Ave,
Walla Walla WA 99362
Ph: 509 529 4685
www.dunhamcellars.com

8. **Gamache Vintners** PAGE 252
505 Cabernet Court, Prosser WA 99350
Ph: 509 786 7800
www.gamachevintners.com

9. **Gilbert Cellars** PAGE 203
5 North Front St, Yakima WA 98901
Ph: 509 249 9049
www.gilbertcellars.com

10. **Hightower Cellars** PAGE 27
19418 E 583 PR NE,
Benton City WA 99320
Ph: 509 588 2867
www.hightowercellars.com

11. **Maryhill Winery** PAGE 207
9774 Hwy 14, Goldendale WA 98620
Ph: 509 773 1976
www.maryhillwinery.com

12. **Northwest Cellars** PAGE 224
11909 124th Ave NE,
Kirkland WA 98034
Ph: 425 825 9463
www.northwestcellars.com

13. **Pepper Bridge Winery** PAGE 264
1704 J.B. George Rd,
Walla Walla WA 99362
Ph: 509 525 6502
www.pepperbridge.com

14. ***Preston Premium Wines*** PAGE 150
502 E Vineyard Drive, Pasco WA 99301
Ph: 509 545 1990
www.prestonwines.com

15. ***Terra Blanca Winery and Estate Vineyard*** PAGE 267
34715 North Demoss Rd,
Benton City WA 99320
Ph: 509 588 6082
www.terrablanca.com

16. ***Thurston Wolfe Winery*** PAGE 258
588 Cabernet Court, Prosser WA 99350
Ph: 509 786 3313
www.thurstonwolfe.com

17. ***Walter Dacon Wines*** PAGE 82
50 SE Skookum Inlet Rd,
Shelton WA 98584
Ph: 360 426 5913
www.walterdaconwines.com

18. ***Waterbrook Winery*** PAGE 260
10518 West Highway 12,
Walla Walla WA 99362
Ph: 509 522 1262
www.waterbrook.com

19. ***Wawawai Canyon*** PAGE 257
5602 State Route 270,
Pullman WA 99163
Ph: 509 338 4916
www.wawawaicanyon.com

20. ***Zerba Cellars*** PAGE 209
14525 148th Ave NE,
Woodinville WA 98077
Ph: 425 806 2749
www.zerbacellars.com

WINE DOGS BREED INDEX

THANK YOU...

Wine Dogs would like to thank the following people who helped us on our journey.

To our wonderful network of friends and family back in Australia whose constant support and enthusiasm has made this book a lot easier to produce. The production of this title was made more difficult by the loss of our last two beloved huskies. The 18-year legacy that our three huskies, Tok, Tarka and Stella have left us will always be treasured. We miss them every day.

Along our travels we were helped and encouraged by many wonderful people including: Roger and Priscilla Higgins at Three Creek Vineyard; Garret and Kim Murphy, Andy Renda the gang at the Vintners Collective Napa Valley; the dynamic Chris Parker from St Supéry; Pat and Robert Parker; Angela Downer Moench and Howard Moench at Stone House Vineyards; Hailey and Janet Trefethen at Trefethen Family Vineyards; Jean-Charles Boisset at Raymond Vineyards, Sam Baxter and Coben Alexander at Terra Valentine Winery; Jim and Joanne Dunham at Dunham Cellars, Vailia Esh and Russell From at Herman Story Wines, Brian and Claudia Fleury at Fleury Estate Winery; Paul LaRose at the Bounty Hunter; Sally Ottoson at Pacific Star Winery; Nicole Marino from Big Shot in Wine Country; Thomas Keller at The French Laundry; Sandra Nicholas at Red Hook; Amelia Moran Ceja and Barbara Russack at Ceja Vineyards; Vern and Maxine Boltz at Toulouse Vineyards; Mary Colhoun at Landmark Vineyards; David Morrisette, Mechelle O'Neal and Rachel van Luik at Chateau Morrisette; Steve Dresler at Sierra Nevada Brewery; Buff, Ernie and the splendid people at Buffalo Shipping Post in Napa. A big thank you to all the very generous wineries that gave us bottles of their fine wine to bring back to Australia. It's a real treat for us Aussies to taste what the other side of the world is drinking.

And we must draw special attention to the wonderful generosity and hospitality offered to us by Margrit Mondavi. We really appreciate your support, kindness and friendship.

When in Napa Valley, Wine Dogs recommends you stay at the amazing Napa River Inn located in the very heart of Napa town. Stunning rooms and pet-friendly, it's within staggering distance of many fine restaurants and wine bars. Many thanks to Lisa Koester for making our exhausting travels less stressful.

Our visit to Oregon was highlighted by our stay at Joan Davenport's Wine Country Farm in Dayton. Heralded as one of the 1,000 places in the world you must see before you die, this Inn is sensational, and Joan's hospitality seemed like nothing was too much bother. Breathtaking views and Joan's superb breakfasts made it very difficult to move on. Thanks for looking after us, Joan, and we can't wait to come back.

Special thanks too to all our contributors: Robert Parker, Cole Danehower, Eve Bushman, Angela Downer Moench, Benjamin Spencer, Vailia Esh, Kelly Davis, Drew Dickson and Greg Duncan Powell for their excellently crafted stories and support. Thanks guys.

To Catherine Rendell for her amazing Wine Dogs website work, Lily Li and Vicky Fisher for helping make Wine Dogs great.

Our apologies to the wineries that we didn't get to visit. Please contact us and we'll be sure to get you in the next edition.

WINE DOGS USA 4

If your winery and woofer missed out on appearing in this edition, please contact us at entries@winedogs.com and register for the Wine Dogs USA 4. We'll look forward to hearing from you. Woof!

IN MEMORY OF ALL OUR BELOVED WINE DOGS